D0364049

THE A TO Z OF GOLF

Written by **Steve Newell**

THE A TO OF
GOLF

This edition first published in the UK in 2009
By Green Umbrella Publishing

© Green Umbrella Publishing 2009

www.gupublishing.co.uk

Publishers Jules Gammond and Vanessa Gardner

Printed and bound in Italy

ISBN: 978-1-906635-27-5

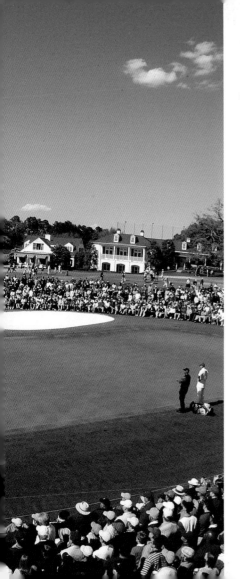

Contents

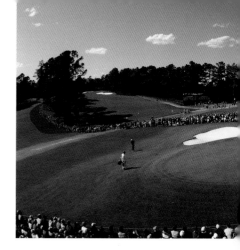

Augusta National

That this is one of only two golf courses to make it into this alphabetical almanac gives you an idea of Augusta National's standing in the game. This isn't the hardest golf course in the world, but it is probably the most beautiful; the 13th hole alone has more than 1,300 azaleas lining fairway and green. And it also happens to play host to one of the biggest and most enthralling tournaments in golf; the Masters.

Despite the fact that today's golf season seemingly has no beginning or end, the Masters is still seen as the curtain-raiser to the golfing year. It being the first of the four major championships serves only to intensify the excitement.

Even the players aren't immune from its intoxicating influence, as Ernie Els says, "Everyone in golf gets excited about the Masters. With it being the first major of the year, you're raring to go and there's this incredible sense of anticipation and excitement. You actually need to try to calm yourself down a bit for the first round on Thursday!"

Intriguingly, Augusta National is something of a paradox. The club's reputation for exclusivity gives it an aura of mystery; its colonial-style, white clubhouse is impenetrable to all but the privileged, and yet because the Masters returns every year there is also an element of familiarity that simply doesn't exist

at many tournament venues.

For fans, it's the hardest ticket in golf. It makes finals day on Centre Court at Wimbledon look like open house. It's no pushover for players either. The only guarantee of getting an invite back in future years is to win the tournament. A quick poll among some of the great players to have achieved this feat, gives an indication of what it means, and also hints at the charm this place exudes.

Phil Mickelson, champion in 2004, could not contain his excitement when he finally got his hands on the famed Green Jacket. In the post-tournament interview in the Butler Cabin he said to Augusta Chairman Hootie Johnson, "you'll have to get used to seeing my mug (face) here forever because I'm always coming back".

Nick Faldo, three-time champion, says, "Augusta National is quite simply one of the most beautiful places in the world. Every year I really look forward to sitting on the veranda of the clubhouse and breathing in the unique atmosphere."

Gary Player, another three-time champion, says, "The minute you drive in the gates you begin to choke up. The Masters has a special time and place in my life. The place oozes atmosphere. The back nine is the greatest in golf."

◀ Stewart Cink and Tiger Woods play the ninth hole during the final round of the 2008 Masters Tournament at Augusta.

▼ Gary Player sinks the putt that wins the 1961 Masters.

Arnold Palmer, four-time champion in the space of seven years, says, "I love Augusta National. It is the perfect place to play golf. The golf course is perfect, the greens, the fairways, the food, the people, everything."

The mighty Jack Nicklaus, a winner six times during a period that spanned an incredible 24 years, has this to say, "The Masters is a monument to everything that is great in golf. The mystique about Augusta National is Bob Jones and what he meant to golf, the class with which the event is run, and all the other special things you just won't find in any other place. It's a cut above, way above."

Bob Jones, its co-founder and one of the greatest golfers who ever lived (see Quadrilateral, later in this book), perhaps best summed up the nature of the challenge, "There isn't a single hole out there that can't be birdied if you just think. But there isn't one that can't be double-bogeyed if you ever stop thinking."

Which is partly why during its 75-year history the vibrant green backdrop of Augusta National has become a theatre of triumph and disaster. There are bigger numbers on this golf course, especially on the back nine, than maybe any other tournament venue in golf.

Tom Weiskopf dumped six balls in the creek at the front of the 12th green on the way to a breakdown-inducing 13; that's 10 over par on one hole, folks. Tommy Nakajima also made a 13 on the par-5 13th in 1974, while in 1987 fellow Japanese, Jumbo Ozaki, racked up an 11 on the 15th, a hole that saw 10 eights or worse in 1998. The role call of shame goes on and on, but you get the idea. Further endorsing Augusta's reputation as a dangerous place for golfers, its worst eclectic score – in other words, the highest score registered on each hole in tournament play – is 163, a staggering 91 over par.

It was scoring of a sublime nature, however, which put Augusta National and the Masters tournament on the map. Bobby Jones' unpretentious invitational tournament had been going for only a couple of years when little Gene Sarazen popped up and created his own bit of history.

Standing on the tee of the par-5 15th, Sarazen was three shots behind the leader Craig Wood. After a solid drive down the middle, Sarazen was sizing up his treacherous second shot over water and, pondering for a moment, heard his playing partner Walter Hagen encouraging him to get a move on because he had "a dinner date tonight". Sarazen took the hint. He promptly reached for his 4-wood and struck the shot sweetly; the ball carried the water hazard, pitched on the front of the green and rolled into the cup for that rarest of birds – an albatross-two.

There were but a few spectators watching, no doubt in amazement, but it was soon dubbed "the shot heard around the world". Sarazen had caught the leaders with one extraordinary stroke and went on to win the tournament in a 36-hole play-off against Craig Wood the next day.

Within a few years the Masters ranked alongside the Open Championship, US Open, and US PGA Championship as one of golf's prestigious four major championships, its Green Jacket, awarded to the winner each year, every bit as famous as the Open's Claret Jug.

Multiple Masters winners through the ages reads like a who's who of the world's dominant golfers – Byron Nelson (two wins), Sam Snead (three), Ben Hogan (two), Arnold Palmer (four), Jack Nicklaus (six), Gary Player (three), Tom Watson (two), Seve Ballesteros (two), Nick Faldo (three) and Tiger Woods (four). It seems to bring out the best in the best.

Amazingly, the course itself changed very little in its first 65 or so years. When it opened for play in 1933, it measured 6,700 yards; as recently as 2001 it had only grown to 6,985 yards – or around four paces a year – a tribute to the skills of its architect Dr Alister MacKenzie.

Only in recent years have improvements in club and ball technology prompted the "Men of the Masters" to add serious length with

◀ Arnold Palmer celebrates winning the Masters, 1960.

▼ Bobby Jones, co-founder of Augusta (left) and Gene Sarazen.

the latest 155-yard increase taking the course up to 7,445 yards for the 2006 Masters. Inevitable progress to some; tinkering with the sacred to others. Either way Augusta's powers-that-be simply do not want their fabled course humiliated by power hitting.

"Tiger-proofing" is a term that has been bandied about to justify these changes, but many feel it just plays into his hands even more by making it even harder for shorter hitters. It certainly didn't stop him winning Green Jacket number four in a thrilling 2005 Masters after a play-off with American, Chris DiMarco – no long hitter yet a bit of an Augusta specialist himself.

Thankfully, Augusta National's other intricacies ensure it will never be a golf course for the faint-hearted. Nowhere is the margin for error so tiny. As Tiger Woods said himself, "You know you can hit one simple shot that catches a slope, one foot away from being a good shot, and the next thing you know you are looking at probably making a bogey or double bogey."

Or put another way, by two-time champion Ben Crenshaw, "...they give you plenty of rope to hang yourself".

Perhaps just as well, then, that they don't let the public go and play!

► Tiger Woods tees off at the fifth in the 2003 Masters.

Ball

Without the invention of the ball, golf wouldn't be called golf. It would be known simply as "walk". And where's the challenge in that? Okay, we'd all do well in a championship for pretty-looking practice swings, but one imagines the novelty would surely have soon worn off.

Enough idle speculation, though. Let's chart the golf ball's truly remarkable journey, one that has been nothing short of mind-boggling even accepting that every single aspect of golf has developed at an incredible pace in the last 100 years or so.

When the likes of Allan Robertson, universally recognised as golf's first ever professional, and his cronies were playing the game with such distinction around the early to mid-19th century, the ball consisted of, unbelievably, boiled goose feathers stuffed into a leather pouch which was then stitched together and fashioned into a shape vaguely spherical.

When the weather and ground conditions were dry, this so-called "feathery" was just about playable. Although quite frankly, the quality of the scoring almost defies belief when one also takes into account the primitive clubs that were used and the unkempt nature of the terrain that passed as a

▶ Some of the more bizarre early irons.

▶▶ The Haskell ball transformed the game at the beginning of the 20th century.

▼ Two early featheries, circa 1850.

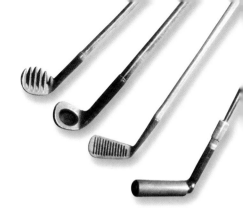

typical golf course in that era.

When it was wet, though, the ball's playing characteristics became so unfathomable as to be almost comical. Not quite a hit and hope, but close. You think hitting a straight shot is difficult nowadays. Back then, a wet golf ball rendered it all but impossible.

The arrival of the gutta percha ball in the mid 19th century signalled the end of the feathery. Sadly for Allan Robertson, it was the end of his livelihood, too, which revolved in every sense around the business of making and selling featheries from his pro shop by the side of the 18th green on St Andrews' Old Course.

Robertson's declining fortunes were in marked contrast to those of the game, however, and golf thrived as never before. The "guttie" as it became known, was manufactured from the rubber-like substance sourced from the percha tree. It was considerably cheaper to produce compared to the labour-intensive feathery – only a quarter of the price – and therefore a greater proportion of the population were able to take to the game.

In fact, with no social barriers to act as a deterrent, just about anyone who had even the remotest interest in golf could have a go.

And with some success, because the guttie was light years ahead of the feathery in terms of performance and durability. It was so revolutionary that it actually influenced the way the game was played. The top golfers of the day started to develop swings which generated a much harder hit, no longer restricted by the fragile nature of yesteryear's feathery.

Just a few decades later, the game moved on again when a wealthy American businessman invented a golf ball with a rubber core. Called the "Haskell" after its creator, the ball was even livelier than the guttie and flew considerably further through the air. It

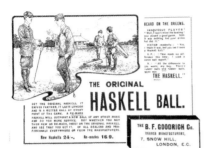

THE ORIGINAL

HASKELL BALL.

GET THE ORIGINAL HASKELL. IT
DRIVES FARTHER, IT LASTS LONGER
AND IS A BETTER BALL AT EVERY
POINT OF THE GAME. A RE-MADE
HASKELL WILL OUTPOINT A NEW BALL OF ANY OTHER MAKE
AND DO YOU MORE SERVICE. BUY WHETHER YOU BUY
THEM NEW OR RE-MADE, INSIST ON THE ORIGINAL HASKELL
AND SEE THAT YOU GET IT. OF ALL DEALERS AND PRO-
FESSIONALS EVERYWHERE OR FROM THE MANUFACTURERS.

New Haskells 24 •.,   Re-mades 16 9.

THE B. F. GOODRICH Co.
RUBBER MANUFACTURERS,
7, SNOW HILL,
LONDON, E.C.

HEARD ON THE GREENS.

VANQUISHED PLAYER : " Well, I can't mind the backing :
buy played a good game. Still
it was nothing but your drives
bat did it."

VICTOR modestly : " Yes,
maybe it was, bat you see I were
a Haskell ball."

V.P. : "Shot made no dif-
ference this time. I used a
comet ball myself."

V. : " All the difference in
the world, my boy. There's
rubber balls and rubber balls,
mind you —

THE HASKELL."

also enabled golfers to manufacture a
wider range of shots, controlling both
the flight and spin of the ball.

Today we take golf balls very much
for granted. They are uniform in shape
and – assuming you can keep them for
long enough – remarkably durable.
The ball's actual dimensions are strictly
monitored by golf's governing bodies.
It must be at least 1.68" in diameter,
weigh no more than 1.62oz, and have
an initial velocity not exceeding 250
feet per second.

But these restrictions haven't held it
back with modern high-performance
models meeting the golfer's seemingly
incompatible demands of distance, feel,
control and durability better than ever
before – a Utopian combination simply
not available in one small white dimpled
sphere a few short years ago. The rule

makers have become increasingly
concerned in light of
unprecedented distance gains
this century – at least among
Tiger and his tour chums –
even writing to manufacturers
politely requesting
prototypes designed to
go shorter distances for
"research purposes".
Whether that ultimately
leads to anything remains
to be seen. They may feel
the ball is going too far, but
for the majority of amateurs, golf
ball technology has had only positive
implications.

On a lighter note, coloured balls
have been around for ages, but the latest
breed from Maxfli and others feature
transparent covers that allow coloured
cores to shine through, bringing pastel
limes, tangerines and raspberries to the
fairways – a welcome
chance to liven things
up when your
game itself is an
unpalatable shade of
grey. Sadly, though,
no one's yet invented
a ball you can't lose.

▲ Gutta percha
balls, circa 1890.

▼ The modern
golf ball such as
the Titleist Pro
V1 is making the
game too easy
(apparently!)

Caddie

The life of the caddie has come a long way from its earthy origins. Go back roughly 100 years and you'd have found them to be a rather feckless company of men, a bit of a rum bunch who, if not gainfully employed on the golf course, could be found hanging around the caddiemaster's hut... or local pub.

Liberating as it might well have been to work outdoors everyday, striding out with a bag of golf clubs over your shoulder, it's hard to believe it was ever a great career move in those days. It was harder then, too. Not only was the money poor, but until the 1930s there was no limit to the number of clubs that a player could stuff into his bag. It was not unheard of for some professionals to go into battle with as many as 25 clubs on board – surely enough to cope with every conceivable shot and

situation the game could throw at them, and definitely enough to give the poor caddie a triple hernia.

Things did improve, thankfully. For starters, the rules were changed to limit the number of clubs a player could carry to just 14, so that lightened the load for the long-suffering bag carrier. More significantly, caddying became recognised as a skilled profession and decent ones were much sought after. They even got recognition from players for a job well done... sometimes.

And so as big money flooded into the pro game, some of it began to

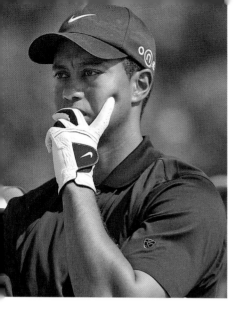

dollars a year. But if your player is missing cuts then you're receiving five per cent of diddly squat. And although caddies receive a basic weekly wage from their boss, it's not nearly enough to cover their expenses which typically include a hotel for, say, five nights, all meals, and of course, the airfare to get there in the first place. You need a very understanding bank manager to sustain that lifestyle for very long. And the fact is, many opt out and decide the caddie's life is not for them.

The definition of a caddie in the Rules of Golf is "...a person who carries or handles a player's clubs during play and otherwise assists him in accordance with the rules". If only it were that simple. On the plus side, professional caddies are no longer required to pace-out the yardages for themselves at each golf course. Instead, they simply purchase a chart from someone else.

On the downside, those die-hard toughies who stick at caddying in the long term must

◀ Steve Jones and Tiger Woods contemplate life in 2004.

▼ Nick and Fannie, at the 2003 Open, have been through the rough and the smooth.

trickle down on to the caddie's table. Tiger's caddie, Steve Williams, was, incredibly, the highest earning Kiwi sports person a year or two ago by virtue of the percentage he gets from the World No.1's winnings. How about that? And these days many caddies hitch a ride in the boss' private jet, standard issue for the elite.

For every caddie who is, as they say, "minting it", there are 50 more who could be described as "slumming it". You see, five or 10 per cent of your boss' winnings is fine and dandy when the guy is raking in several million

wonderfully the emotional tightrope a caddie walks between first tee and 18th green. The episode occurred at a European Tour event when he was caddying for the hardworking journeyman pro Peter Teravainen.

This was not your typical tour pro. Teravainen's swing was so violent that it earned the nickname "Whiplash" among many of his contemporaries; indeed, such was the physical effort he put into the swing he once fainted in his follow-through, spraining his arm in the fall. Teravainen was caught in a fashion time warp and was very much his own man, a self-taught individual who spurned the accoutrements of the typical pro. He had no coach, no agent, no clothing contract (obviously!) and not even a sports psychologist – although judging by his occasional behaviour he might have been wise to engage the services of such a fellow.

contend with far more than simply the vagaries of an unreliable income stream. There's the psychological roller coaster to consider.

This is part and parcel of most caddies' lives. Once again, it's a virtual walk in the park when your player is shooting 65s and winning tournaments. It can seem easy then. Although saying that, it takes bottle to give advice to a pro golfer. God help you if you chirp up at a crucial moment, "no boss, definitely take the 5-iron, not the 6-iron" and it proves wrong advice.

The implications are dire for a caddie's well-being. In his terrific book *To The Linksland*, author and journalist Michael Bamberger describes

No wonder Bamberger picked out this man from the crowd when he set out to experience the caddie's life. Here, surely, would be a rich source of material. He was not to be disappointed. Bamberger should have spotted what was coming when he was reprimanded early in their partnership that the clubs were rattling too much in the bag when he walked.

A few weeks later, in the Italian Open, Bamberger innocently cried "sit down, golf ball", as a Teravainen chip shot showed no sign of slowing down as it slid past the hole. The golf ball, not having ears, continued to roll and eventually toppled into a greenside bunker. Teravainen was visibly unamused and went on to make bogey, on a par-5 of all holes, a crime in pro golf. As they walked off the green, Teravainen turned to Bamberger and yelled, "never talk to my golf ball, never talk to my golf ball, goddamnit, never talk to my golf ball".

It was, apparently, a rare moment of meanness and on the whole, Bamberger enjoyed his time with Teravainen. But it served to illustrate one thing that most caddies have to accept as part of the job; that when things start to go pear-shaped, the person on the receiving end of a player's anger and frustration will usually be the one closest to them, the caddie.

There are dozens of other caddies with similar tales to tell, like Bamberger's, of being the innocent victim of a ferocious tongue lashing.

Equally, there are many more who wouldn't dream of doing anything else to earn a living. Some develop a relationship with the player which extends way beyond the boss/employee dimension and into the realms of true friendship.

Take Tom Watson and his caddie Bruce Edwards, who sadly passed away during Masters week 2004. Together they won countless tournaments and even a major championship, Edwards forever the loyal caddie by Watson's side. A few years ago Edwards was diagnosed as suffering from a rare and tragically debilitating illness, and throughout that traumatic period Watson did everything he could to return that loyalty, including paying Edwards' medical bills and funding research into trying to find a cure for the condition. It speaks volumes for the character of Watson and also for the depth of the friendship they developed "inside the ropes".

◀ Unorthodox American Peter Teravainen.

▼ Bruce Edwards acknowledges the well-wishers at the 2003 US Open.

Divot

Ah, the humble divot. Nothing more than a clod of earth really. Or, from certain angles, John Daly's style of haircut in the early 1990s. Whatever, the divot doesn't seem to get a lot of attention. Even the lucky few who are picked up and replaced get stamped on. Poor sods!

Good and bad shots alike can result in a divot being taken. This creates a lot of confusion, especially among beginners who often toil away under the mistaken belief that the ball should be struck, clean-as-a-whistle, leaving not so much as a blemish on the manicured fairway. As we'll learn, that is indeed the case with some shots. But not all shots.

The interesting thing about divots ...well, maybe not interesting, but revealing, is that they can tell you a lot about your golf swing. You just need to know how to read the signs. So here's a quick lesson in the hitherto unheralded art of "divot recognition". They don't teach you this at school.

In actual fact, it's not so much the divot you need to study, but the hole left in the ground after the divot has left the scene. If it points left of the target, the indisputable fact is you are swinging

you're swinging the club through the hitting zone on an exaggerated in-to-out path. You'll tend to hit a lot of shots which either start right and stay right, or start right and swerve violently from right-to-left through the air. All depends how lively you are with your hands. Either way, it's not desirable.

A divot hole which points straight at the target is what you might call the "Holey Grail" of golf, because it suggests a swing path which corresponds exactly with the direction you want the ball to start. Obviously a plus point. Any subsequent deviation in the ball's flight can be attributed to poor clubface alignment at impact. If the ball moves to the left, the clubface is closed at impact. If the ball moves to the right, the clubface is open at impact. Just as that little golf ball can be your most discerning teacher, so too can be the divot.

The actual shape of a divot hole can even tell you something

◀ John Daly (left) and David Toms in divot heaven!

▼ Divot pointing left equals shot flying to the left of the target or the dreaded slice.

across the line on an out-to-in path. This will result in shots that fly to the left of the target, mostly with the shorter clubs. If you are using a longer club, the straight face allied to the crooked swing path will result in a slice. Very nasty, as we'll learn later in the book.

If your divot hole points right of target, the opposite problem applies;

about the suitability, or otherwise, of your equipment. The start of the divot hole – in other words, the exact point where the leading edge of the clubhead first makes contact with the ground – should be square. That is, perpendicular to the target line. This is a sign that the clubhead is flush to the ground when it meets the ball. It will therefore be less prone to twisting at impact, the cause of many stray shots.

If that's not the case, and there is a distinctly oblique angle at the entry point of the divot hole, this indicates that the toe or the heel of the club is making contact with the ground prematurely. That's the sign of an ill-suited set of irons and, make no mistake, that's bound to cause you problems with the quality of your shot making. Make an appointment straight away with your local professional, who can adjust the lie-angle of your irons to suit your posture and swing.

Even the absence of a divot hole can speak volumes. With short irons, where a slightly descending angle of attack is essential for solid contact, a divot should always be taken. The perfect strike is, in essence, a ball-then-turf affair. The divot shouldn't be a huge, doormat proportioned slab of earth, but it should be a divot nonetheless. If that isn't happening when you play a short-iron approach shot into a green, there's something amiss in your technique. It might only be something as elementary as incorrect ball position in your set up, but it needs addressing anyway.

And, you probably guessed it, taking a divot isn't always a good thing. The longer clubs in your bag, from the driver all the way down to the 3- and 4-iron, require a shallow angle of attack to produce solid shots. If you're taking a divot of any substance with these clubs, that's a sign your angle of attack into the ball is a little too steep. You're allowed a slight bruising of the turf; that, you can get away with. But more than that means you need to take a look at your technique and make a change for the better.

And hey, don't neglect that poor divot. Always replace it after every shot, as that way nature will ensure the

As Phil Mickleson shows, you should always take a divot with your short irons.

Not the result you want to see with a 3-iron.

fairway repairs itself. The greenkeeper will love you and the fairways at your club will be less inclined to bear the scars of wear and tear. And let's not forget, if everyone adhered to this simple procedure, you'd never again endure the frustration and depression of hitting a drive straight down the middle of the fairway, only to find the ball has come to rest in an old divot hole.

Etiquette

W hat a thoroughly agreeable term "etiquette" is. Very old school. When one describes the game of golf as being blessed with good etiquette, it makes you think of a game for gentlemen, of "jolly good eggs" playing a swift 18 before elevenses and partaking in a few ginger beer shandies in the bar afterwards.

Sure does shatter the illusion a bit when you turn on the television and see a leading professional spit a mighty gob of phlegm on to a pristine fairway! Lovely.

But come on, let's not dwell on isolated negative incidents. For it remains a source of great pride that standards of behaviour in golf are on an altogether different level when compared to many other sports. With golf you sense that it's as much about how the game is played, as how well it is played. If you practise good etiquette, you can command respect, almost regardless of your ability. Behave like a cretin, though, and even possessing a low single-figure handicap won't gain you many friends or playing partners.

What exactly, then, is good etiquette? Well, without wishing to get too pompous, it describes a high

statement of intent that golf's governing bodies have no desire to see standards slip as they perhaps have done in certain sports.

It's important that golfers treat both fellow players and the course itself with respect if the sport is to retain the moral high ground it currently occupies. And in all truth much of it is common-sense.

Obviously you shouldn't take practice swings within striking distance of your playing companions. Golf is a non-contact sport, remember. So just watch out of the corner of your eye before you go swishing away with your driver.

Also, do not stand in a position where there is even the slightest chance that the ball might hit you. A golf ball is a dangerous missile, travelling in excess of 100mph, so don't take chances. The correct place to stand is slightly to the right and behind the angle of play, which has the added benefit of being out of the player's line

◄ An immaculately attired gentleman tees off at the 18th at St Andrews.

▼ Golfers on mobiles on the course are guaranteed to annoy their playing partner and everyone else in earshot.

moral code of personal integrity and good behaviour. Such is its importance that the Rules of Golf dedicates four full pages to etiquette advice – and now gives committees the power to disqualify any player found to be in "serious breach of etiquette". An ultimate sanction to be implemented only sparingly, but still a strong of sight. As an added courtesy, you should stand still and be quiet when another player addresses the ball. Don't talk, don't fidget, and certainly don't jangle coins!

Before teeing off, you should be absolutely confident that the golfers in the group in front have moved out of range. Your Sunday best drive will not lead to words of appreciation if the ball whistles past someone's head. It may be frustrating if you are being held up,

but rather than forcing the issue, it's far better to have a polite word on the next tee. If it is appropriate, they should call you through.

Pace of play is another factor falling into the category of courtesy for others. One of the rules of golf states that you must "play without undue delay" and there are penalties for a breach of this rule, as witnessed virtually every week in professional tournaments. At club level these rules are rarely,

▶ Nick Faldo being warned for slow play at the Masters, 1996.

if ever, enforced, which many see as an invitation to play at the proverbial snail's pace. Please, no! All you have to remember is this; keep up with the game in front. If everyone did that, and assuming the first group on the golf course aren't playing at the speed of the aforementioned snail, there would be very few delays. And golf at club level would be blessedly more enjoyable for it. We can live in hope.

Finally, help your fellow competitor in the search for golf balls. You'd appreciate the same courtesy when you next struggle to find your ball in the rough, or wherever. Remember you've got only five minutes to find it, though. At that point, you have to declare it lost and proceed accordingly.

As for looking after the golf course, the second aspect of good etiquette, again common sense features

▲ Even the greats – Els, Price and Woods in this case – help each other look for lost balls.

▲ A golfer's nightmare – always rake the bunker.

▶ Two releases from David Leadbetter and Ernie Els.

bit of gardening not only spares another golfer from the misery of having to play a shot from an old divot hole, it helps the fairway repair itself far more quickly and without blemish.

The same principle applies to the putting green. If your approach shot lands on the green leaving an indentation or pitch mark, repair it the moment you set foot on the green and another while you're at it, because you can be sure that some other golfer has forgotten how to look after the course... or doesn't care.

Finally, rake your footprints in the sand after you've finished in a bunker. Let's face it, bunker play is hard enough, without having to extricate your ball from a size-10 footprint. If the rake usually provided for the purpose has gone missing for whatever reason, at least make the best job you can by smoothing over footprints with the clubhead of your sand-wedge. It's a surprisingly effective tool when used in a shallow, sweeping motion.

All of these measures help make the game more enjoyable for everyone and take only a moment's thought. And the other thing is, good etiquette actually soon becomes second nature.

prominently. It's no bad thing to forever keep in mind the old adage that is; if you look after the golf course the golf course will in turn look after you. If this reciprocal arrangement sometimes fails you, perhaps when your flushed drive comes to rest in an old divot, curse not the golf course, but the inconsiderate golfer who failed to replace the divot in the first place.

It should serve as a reminder of one of the most important codes of etiquette; always replace divots after every shot. As we explained in the previous chapter (see Divot) this simple

Faults & Fixes

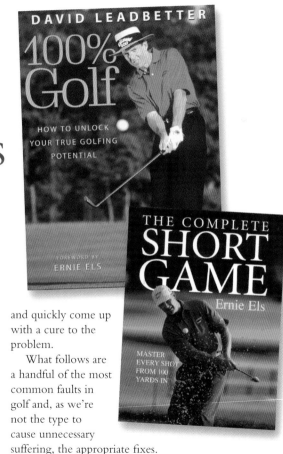

Golf, as you may well have noticed, is not an easy game. That's why the likes of John Jacobs, David Leadbetter, Butch Harmon, and many other high profile teachers before them, make more than a few bob from the instruction books we weekend golfers buy. No harm in that. The quality of golf books on the market is, generally, excellent. And these top teachers know their stuff, all right.

There are times, however, when you don't have access to a book, or a coach. And when, despite your cries to the heavens, divine intervention isn't coming any time soon either. That's when you need a grasp of the law of "Faults and Fixes", in essence the ability to identify what you're doing wrong and quickly come up with a cure to the problem.

What follows are a handful of the most common faults in golf and, as we're not the type to cause unnecessary suffering, the appropriate fixes. The rest is in your hands.

▶ The clubhead is too far away from the body. This will cause a shank.

▶▶ The correct position.

Fault No.1 – The Shank

A shank occurs when the ball is struck out of the neck of the clubhead, at the base of the shaft. That's what creates the nightmarish ball-flight, where it shoots off at right-angles to the line of play... often never to be seen again.

The cause of this ugly shot is simple; the clubhead is further away from your body when the ball is struck, than it was when you addressed it. Think about that. Even though you might set up

with the sweet spot adjacent to the ball, your swing shape is such that the neck of the club is what hits the ball.

The swing path for a shank is usually such that the clubhead swings across the line on an out-to-in path. To eliminate this from your game, try to feel that your hands and arms swing the club down from the top of the swing, before the shoulders begin to unwind. So, arms first, then body. That gets the club on an inside path into impact, which is much less likely to cause a shank. You might even try to consciously hit shots out of the toe. That slight overcompensation often gets you finding the sweet spot again. And you can't hit a shank from there!

Fault No.2 – Mis-hitting Putts

The single biggest cause of mis-hit putts is a crooked stroke; it's as simple as that. With the putter-head not travelling on a consistent and true path, you have no hope of hitting the ball consistently out of the same part of the putter-face. On one green you'll leave a putt short, then on the next green you'll boom it eight feet past the hole. It will, in the time-honoured golfing vernacular, "do your head in".

The secret lies in training yourself to make an on-line stroke, so you make contact with the sweet spot more consistently. A simple drill to help you achieve this involves placing two tee-pegs in the ground, about half-an-inch either side of the heel and toe of your putter. Address the ball on the sweet spot, then swing the putter back and through. The idea is that you strike the ball without the putter touching either tee-peg. If you make a crooked stroke, you'll knock over one or both of the tee-pegs.

◀ The perfect crooked stroke will result in a perfect poor putt!

▼ A good putting exercise.

► The ball too far back in the stance will often cause a hook.

►► The correct setup position.

With practise, this routine trains you to swing the putter correctly so you strike the ball from where you addressed it – in other words, out of the sweet spot. That's what you're looking for on the golf course, because with a consistent strike comes consistent judgement of distance.

Fault No.3 – The Hook

Some say a hook is the good player's bad shot, which actually does have an element of truth about it. But these sentiments are of no consolation as you watch your ball veer left into the trees. By definition the hook shot must start right of the target. The ball then curves from right-to-left through the air. Its close sibling is the push, which shares many of the same swing traits. So one of the benefits of curing your hook is you don't hit as many push shots, either. Excellent!

Why does the ball start right? Because the ball is too far back in the stance. It almost forces you to swing the club on an in-to-out path. Why does the ball then swerve from right-to-left? Well, that in-to-out path requires a lot of hand action to prevent the ball flying miles right, which results in the clubface

closing. That's what imparts sidespin on the ball, hence the hook. The push simply comes about when you don't close the clubface in time.

To shake off the hook, move the ball up in your stance, opposite your

line path into the back of the ball. It's almost an instinctive reaction, rather than a conscious action. As a result, the ball starts on target.

Fault No.4 – Hitting Shots Heavy
Somewhat depressingly, you can hit a shot heavy with almost any club in the bag. The clubhead gouges into the turf before it meets the ball so you get a cushioned impact, as it were. You won't lose many golf balls, because the ball doesn't fly far enough. As with most bad shots, the problem stems from a poor set up, borne from a desire to try to help the ball into the air. The ball is usually too far forward in the stance and the weight hangs back on the right side during the swing in an effort to scoop the ball into the air, which causes the arc of the swing to "bottom out" before the clubhead actually reaches the ball.

The key is to set up in such a way that your weight is evenly spread and the ball is placed correctly in your stance, not too far forward. Then let your weight flow in the direction of the swinging clubhead, to help "centre" the arc of your swing and therefore collect the ball cleanly.

left heel. That alone addresses most of the problems. For a start, your shoulders are aligned correctly, not closed. More significantly, it encourages the correct swing path through the hitting area. The club more naturally follows an on-

▲ An angry reaction after a dreadful topped drive.

Fault No.5 – Topped Drive

Not getting the ball airborne is just pathetic, right up there at the top of the embarrassment stakes. But we've all done it. Stood on the first tee, any tee for that matter, and stone-cold topped the ball along the ground. More often than not it's caused by chopping down too steeply on to the ball.

The tell tale signs are usually there at address, with the weight favouring the front foot slightly, the ball a little too far back in the stance. In the backswing,

the weight then gets stuck on the left side – the reverse of what should happen. It's then all too easy to let it stay there in the downswing. The angle of attack becomes excessively steep and, with the ball too far back in the stance, a topped drive is inevitable.

The fixing process, as always, starts at address. Get the weight nicely settled on the right side, the ball further forward in the stance, positioned as it should be opposite the left heel. From there it's so much easier to load your weight into your right side and get behind the ball at the top of the backswing. And that's where you need to be, in order to sweep the ball away with a shallow blow. And you won't top it like that. You'll make dead solid contact, right out of the sweet spot.

The observant among you will have perhaps noticed that the "slice" does not feature in this list. There's a reason for that. Such is the prevalence of this ghastly shot, that we felt it warranted an inclusion in this book all of its own. It's a shame to give the game away so early, but that's what you'll find under the letter "S". We sincerely hope its entry on these pages offers blessed relief to all sufferers.

Grip

The grip is, without even the slightest shadow of a doubt, the most important fundamental in golf. The great Ben Hogan once said, "a player with a bad grip doesn't want a good golf swing". Always known for his brevity, Hogan hit the nail on the head with this statement.

And yet it is astonishing how little attention is given by most amateurs to this aspect of their technique. Okay, on the face of it, the grip isn't an exciting subject. Found as it is at the start of any instruction book, it's a fair bet that most readers gloss over that section and skip straight to the part which promises "massive distance" or "more power".

But this isn't an instruction book. You won't find any advice in here to help you hit the ball 700 yards off the tee. Let's assume we have your undivided attention. Good. The next

▲ Ben Hogan demonstrating his strong grip for woods and irons.

600 or so words might change your golfing life, forever.

Your hands are your only point of contact with the club, that's the first point worth stressing. Sounds obvious, but it's easy to overlook the implications of this simple phrase. How you grip the club determines the positioning of the clubface during the swing and, crucially, at impact. And obviously it follows that the positioning of the clubface

▲ Old Tom Morris sporting the original baseball grip.

how the game was played in its early years. All the major names of this period – the likes of Allen Robertson and Old Tom Morris – used this method. In actual fact, it was more out of necessity than choice. The grips of clubs were so thick that there was really no other sensible method other than to hold the club in the palm of both hands.

But as the game developed around the early part of the 20th century, a new breed of players began to recognise that there were better ways to grip a golf club. And equipment evolved, which accelerated the wind of change. Basically, the theory was that the hands should be linked in some way, as that would encourage them to work as a more cohesive unit, rather than independently of one another which could prove counterproductive.

And so the overlapping grip came to the fore, whereby the little finger of the right hand would ride piggyback on top of the forefinger of the left hand. The great Harry Vardon was widely recognised as being the inspiration for this grip, hence it is also known as the Vardon grip. But in actual fact, players like J H Taylor (another Open champion) and Leslie Balfour Melville,

determines the initial direction, and subsequent shape, of your golf shots. Everything else you do is of secondary importance, to be honest.

There are three basic types of grip. The baseball, or two-handed grip, represented conventional wisdom on

had already used it with great success. Whatever the origins, the grip used by these players would not look at all out of place in a leading professional tournament in the 21st century.

The third and final accepted variation is the interlocking grip, whereby the little finger of the right hand is entwined with the forefinger of the left. As with the overlapping grip, this encourages the hands to work in harmony during the swing. It is not as widely adopted as the overlapping, or Vardon grip. However, Jack Nicklaus

and Tiger Woods both prefer it. Not a shabby recommendation, it must be said. If you're looking for more concrete reasons to adopt this grip, it is considered preferable for those with relatively small hands, so that might be something to bear in mind if you're not certain which way to go.

Whichever of the three grips you adopt, this quick, three-step guide to forming the perfect golf grip should assist you greatly in making sure the positioning of the hands is correct. It will not, repeat not, feel comfortable straight away. In fact, the first time you try to hit a shot it will feel plain

▲ Tiger Woods favours the interlocking grip.

◀ Harry Vardon demonstrating his grip.

awkward. That can last for hours, days, even weeks, depending on how often you play or practice.

You can reduce the "bedding-in" period if you keep a club close to hand in your house and, every now and then, pick it up and practise your perfect hold. Waggle the club back and forth a little. Just try to get used to the feel of the club in your hands. It is worth persevering, because the benefit of a good grip comes in the shape of a better golf swing and

more consistent, high-quality golf shots. Honestly, can you say that isn't more than a little bit appealing?

1. Align the clubface straight at the target, bring your left hand forward into its natural hanging position, and then feed the club into your hands so it runs diagonally across your palm from the base of your forefinger to the fleshy pad at the top of the palm of your hand. Close your fingers around the grip, making sure your thumb sits just to the right of the centre of the grip. As you look down,

The perfect grip sequence.

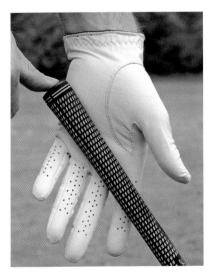

you should now see two-and-a-bit knuckles on the back of your hand.

2. The thing to remember about your right hand hold is that the palm should effectively mirror the position of the clubface – in other words, facing the target. So keeping that in mind, bring your right hand towards the club and feed the grip into your hand, along the base of your middle two fingers.

3. Now close your fingers around the grip. You should feel that your forefinger assumes a kind of "trigger position" pinched in towards

the thumb, which should run diagonally down the left side of the grip. How you knit your hands together is a matter of personal preference, as we described above. As you look down, you should see two knuckles on the back of your right hand.

This is what's described as a neutral hold on the club. It's the perfect grip to allow a free-swinging release of the club, with no conscious manipulation required. That's the way you want to hit your golf shots. It's how you generate the most speed.

Handicap

It's become something of a habit among golf aficionados to rattle out the old argument about how golf's handicapping system allows players of all abilities to compete on an even footing, on any golf course in the world.

They'll say how a weekend footballer couldn't have a knock around with the Arsenal team... well, you could, only you'd look foolish. Or how a member of your local tennis club couldn't play a five-setter against Andy Murray. And that with snooker, a handicapping system exists to give everyone a chance against the likes of Ronnie O'Sullivan. Yeah, right. How exactly does one go about winning a snooker game whilst sitting in a chair, watching?

With golf, though, theoretically a high-handicapper could tee it up against, say, Ernie Els at Wentworth and give him a decent game over 18 holes.

"Theoretically" is the critical word in that sentence. Because yes, you could conceivably give Ernie a run for his money. But in reality, it would almost certainly be a hopelessly one-sided affair.

The evidence, alas, is more overwhelming than an avalanche. Let's first consider what Ernie's handicap might be. If we apply the system adopted by amateurs in this country, and calculate a notional handicap based on the Standard Scratch Score (SSS), the

Ernie's average score over the course of a season is usually 68; again, give or take a 10th or so of a shot. Therefore his handicap is plus-7.

Just dwell on that for a moment, if you will. Plus-7. Equate that to your home golf course. Ernie stands on the first tee, effectively "seven down" on the course. He must make seven birdies and no bogeys every time he plays, just to break even on his handicap for the day. And the scary thing is, he does. Week in, week out.

And if you catch him on a good day, which it must be said occurs rather frequently, he'll shoot a lot lower than that. During the Heineken Classic at the awesome Royal Melbourne in Australia in the early part of the 2004 season, Ernie ripped this tough golf course to shreds with a round of 60, 12-under par. His handicap on that day was probably... wait for it, plus-16!

Without wishing to offend the humble weekend golfer, trying to compete with that is as futile as flapping your arms and expecting to take off. Against someone of the class of Ernie, or Vijay Singh, or obviously Tiger, you'll be having the earliest bath in the history of sporting endeavour.

figures will make you weep.

A typical US Tour event takes place on a golf course measuring somewhere between 7,100 and 7,500 yards. The US adopts a "slope" system for handicapping in the amateur game, which is different to ours on this side of the Atlantic, but let's ignore that technicality. The fact is, the equivalent SSS for this type of golf course would probably be in the region of 75 strokes, give or take a half-shot either way.

▲ Ernie Els acknowledges the crowd after a 60 at Royal Melbourne.

▶ The captain of St Andrews tees up in his match to open the 1876 golf season.

of the group, usually based on three-quarters of the difference in handicap. So for instance, a golfer playing off a handicap of 14, against a 2-handicapper, will receive 10 shots (three-quarters of the difference in handicap, 12, equals 10 shots) which he'll get on the holes with a stroke index between one and 10. On each of those holes, a par for the 14-handicapper is as good as the 2-handicapper's birdie.

But let's not knock the handicapping system and say it is without merit, because nothing could be farther from the truth. At club level it is, indeed, one of the key factors which makes golf such a wonderful, enduring, captivating game.

You can get together with your chums on a Saturday morning for a friendly fourball, throw up the balls and, however they land, be guaranteed of the prospect of a decent game. It may not always be close, but it is fair. The golfer with the lowest handicap simply gives shots to the other members

And think about those monthly medals. Only two divisions are usually required to separate an entire playing membership, typically those with a handicap of 14 and below, and those of 15 and above. That's a big spread in each division. And every single golfer has an equal chance. Try that at a tennis club... well, try it and see what percentage of competitors actually has even half-a-chance of winning.

And in other competitions, the so-called "biggies" where names in gold paint on the honours board are at stake and the playing divisions are usually merged into one, the guy playing off 18 has as much chance of taking home the cup as the guy playing off two. It is a totally level playing field. It's fantastic.

Occasionally, the handicapping system in the UK gets criticised. But, for the time being it's the best system there is. Until someone comes up with something which is evidently better, and no one yet has, we're stuck with it. And thank heavens for that.

▲ A group wait their tee-off before the Hoebridge Golf Course Monthly Medal.

Instruction

▶ Nick Faldo and David Leadbetter at Augusta. Leadbetter now has coaching academies throughout the world.

▼ An early 1962 cover from *Golf World*.

The story of golf instruction is as old as the game itself. It's foolhardy to believe for a second that at least some form of tuition didn't exist in golf's formative years. It's human nature to want to get better, whatever the endeavour. And no game in the history of sport has so inspired its participants to strive for self-improvement. That's the wonderful thing about golf; everyone has the capacity to improve.

Although there is very little documentary evidence in existence to support the widespread use of golf instruction, we do know that as early as 1687 a fellow by the name of Thomas Kincaid wrote in his diary that golfers should "...stand as you do at fencing. Hold the muscles of your legs and back and armes... fixt or stiffe, and not at all slackening them in the time you are bringing down the stroak. Your arms most move but very little; all the motion most be performed with the turning of your body about". Maybe it's best if you don't try that at home!

Progress in golf instruction was swift, marching in time with the growth in popularity of the game among the masses. By the late 19th century, magazines such as *Golf Illustrated* recognised the club golfers' desire for information on how to play better golf, with series' of articles from the leading professionals of the period. It seemed the golfers' thirst for knowledge was

unquenchable and these instructional articles continued to be extremely popular.

That trend in the world of publishing has never once let up in the last 100 years, as advances in photography allowed a degree of swing analysis and coaching simply unavailable to previous generations. In September 1963, *Golf World*'s front cover featured a swing sequence of the young Jack Nicklaus, belting a ball into the distance, teasing the reader into believing, legitimately, that they might be able to learn from the great man's technique.

These days golf magazines all over the world quite literally rely on instruction articles such as this to sell their publications. More often than not, the leading monthly titles feature game improvement-led cover stories. And why not? This formula is a proven

success, for it's a well-researched fact that as many as 70 per cent of readers buy a magazine primarily for the golf instruction. Oh, they'll read the interviews, news stories, course reviews and such like. But their attention can never be diverted for long from the prospect that a tip, a few words of wisdom, will bring them

◀ The leading magazines rely more and more on instruction.

closer to that euphoric state where great golf shots zing from the face of every club in their bag.

The players themselves are enthusiastic collaborators, too. Even as far back as the early 1900s the likes of Harry Vardon, J H Taylor and James Braid – golf's first Great Triumvirate – had come to recognise that golf instruction books could be a lucrative sideline to playing professional golf. A few decades later in the 1930s, when Bobby Jones had won all there was to win and retired from competitive golf,

he helped fill the void by writing a series of best selling golf books. Throughout the 20th century the top players followed suit. Tommy Armour's *How To Play Your Best Golf All The Time* is one of golf's most popular ever instruction books. Ben Hogan's *The Modern Fundamentals of Golf*, published way back in 1957, is still revered as one of the finest golf books ever written. Arnold Palmer, Jack Nicklaus, Sam Snead, Gary Player, Seve Ballesteros, Nick Faldo, and just about every other top player of the last few generations, has cashed in via the world of book publishing.

It's no different now. The world's

best golfers, whilst inordinately wealthier than their counterparts of a century ago and therefore in no need of extra income, still put pen to paper (well, a ghost-writer does that bit!) in the form of instruction books. Some of these books, thoroughly well put together as they are, might be better titled "How I Play Golf" rather than how the reader might improve, for there is no guarantee that what works for one golfer might work for another.

Still, there is merit in most of them – if only for the insight into how a great talent goes about his or her business on the golf course. And if the reader identifies with some of the advice, and is able to integrate it into their own game to help lower their scores, so much the better.

The way the game has been taught historically reflects the techniques employed by the top players of the day. That principle applies from one end of the talent spectrum to the other, in as much that the weekend golfer tries to copy the world's best players, as do the aspiring professional. Everything learned gets passed down through the generations and so the golf swing evolves.

Golf coaches have always played just as significant a role in this development. The golfing guru, the star coach to whom the best players in the world turn, is not a new phenomenon. However, those of yesteryear could not even have dreamed of the success and wealth achieved by many of today's coaches.

John Jacobs, a fine player in his own right who today is revered as one of the greatest teachers of all time, was among the first to raise the profile of the golf coach. He pioneered the concept of the teaching academy and today his golf schools are established all over the United States. Jacobs is as adept at coaching beginners as he is the world's best; everyone benefits from his keen eye and extraordinary gift of communicating complicated swing theories into easily assimilated messages which helped people play better golf, almost straight away. Consequently, many of his instruction books are best sellers.

Some of today's leading gurus, such as David Leadbetter and Butch Harmon, were inspired by Jacobs and have succeeded in their own right to such a degree that they are as famous

as many of the star players they coach. Their names are synonymous with teaching excellence, and it's not just the top players who benefit. The magazine articles and books which come from the likes of Leadbetter, Harmon, and others, have helped millions of golfers all over the world.

As long as golf is played, there'll be a demand for golf coaches. Their words of wisdom, along with the insight provided to us by the top players, guarantees a healthy future for the world of golf instruction. And we'll continue to lap it up because, as we all know, the secret is out there somewhere. If we just keep looking, keep reading, a better golf game is only ever a day away.

▲ John Jacobs coaching José María Olazábal.

◀ Ben Hogan's *The Modern Fundamentals of Golf* first published in 1957.

Journey

The golfer is truly blessed with the variety of playing conditions this game affords us. It's the main reason why thousands, maybe even millions, of golfers travel all over the world to indulge their passion for the game.

Any golfer who has taken a golf holiday will know well the feeling of excitement as you drive in through the gates of the club and set eyes on a new course for the first time. And the sense of anticipation as you walk on to the first tee, a spring in your step, with high expectations of what's ahead. At that moment, you know the journey – no matter how tiresome – was worthwhile.

In this sense, golf is a unique pastime. Let's for a moment compare it with some other sports. Football? Well, in your typical Sunday morning league down at the local park there's no variety at all, really. Most pitches

are the same; very muddy! Okay, in the rarefied world of the Premier League, and such like, not all stadiums are the same. But once on the pitch, the actual playing conditions and dimensions are all much of a muchness. Tennis? Well, the best courts in the world have a certain character, an atmosphere, which is special. Take the Centre Court at Wimbledon; top players say there's nothing else like it. But again, aside from the differences in playing surface, there's not exactly a lot of variety. Especially not at club level. And cricket is the same. So is rugby. And don't even mention snooker!

But with golf you get more variety

Or staring at a tropical forest with monkeys sneaking on to the fairway to steel your golf ball. Or striding out on the springy fairways in a beautifully tranquil heathland setting, with heather and gorse in full bloom. Golf, more than any other pastime, is a sensory bombardment.

Weather plays a huge part, too. Part of the reason we travel is to enjoy a game of golf with the sun on our backs. And whether we enjoy everything that Mother Nature throws at us, that's open for debate. But you can't deny it adds greatly to the experience. Not convinced? How about the challenge of playing a links golf course on a windy day? It completely shatters your perceptions of how far you hit each club. One minute you're playing a

◀ The spectacular Ile Aux Cerfs Golf Course in Trou d'Eau Douce, Mauritius.

▼ The par 4 fifth hole at Royal St Georges Golf Club links course.

than the Pick "n" Mix at Woolworths. No two courses are the same. And if you look at each of the core elements that make up the overall design of the course, the variety is staggering. The general topography of the landscape, the conditions underfoot, the types of grass, the indigenous plants and wildlife, the different shapes and type of bunker, the speed of greens, the length of the course. We could go on, but you get the idea. The list is endless.

Then there's the location. On one golf course you can stand on a tee, take two steps backwards and fall into the ocean! On another, you could be in a green oasis in the middle of a desert.

▲ Different hazards await the golfer abroad, be they monkeys in Malaysia or alligators in Myrtle Beach.

Beware of Alligators

par-3, of a yardage which suggests an easy mid-iron, but into the teeth of a gale requires a full-blooded driver. The next minute, when the direction of play changes, you can be hitting a driver and a wedge on to a par-5, and feeling like a tour pro. You just can't put a price on that kind of experience. It's just fantastically engaging.

Golf travel is a booming business. In fact, golf travel spending is the fastest growth area in the worldwide golf market, growing on average at a rate of nine per cent per annum. In the US alone, golf travel spending exceeds $25 billion a year. All the demographic research in recent years suggests that golfers are a fairly cash-rich bunch. Indeed, something like only one in 10 say money is a determining factor when it comes to pursuing their passion for golf.

Time is the only obstacle for the majority of golfers. Most, indeed nearly all, would love to travel more to play golf. Trouble is, work gets in the way. Not surprisingly then, mini-breaks visiting one particular area and playing a couple of golf courses in the space of two or three days, are especially popular. If you're a Brit, the golfing travel hotspots tend to be

Spain, Portugal, Scotland, Ireland, and France. These countries are just a short hop away on a low cost airline and, once you've chosen a suitable base, you can usually play a bunch of great golf courses if you wish, within a half hour's drive of your hotel.

Of course, for the longer golf holiday it's impossible to beat the United States, where the term "spoilt for choice" takes on a whole new perspective. In Florida alone there are more than 1,300 golf courses. In California there are well over 1,000. Look at the US as a whole and you can take your pick from nearly 20,000 golf courses. That's pretty amazing, even for a big country. And with levels of service, not to mention facilities that put most European golf resorts in the shade, the US has

◀ La Manga in Spain is a popular venue for British golfers as Wayne Rooney and Michael Owen prove.

something of a magnetic pull for golfers.

All of these factors come together and lure us into making that journey. Books have been written on the strength of such dreams. We return again to Michael Bamberger's classic book *To The Linksland* and a passage in which he describes perfectly the magic involved in making a pilgrimage to, and then playing, a great golf course. In this case, the course was Royal Dornoch in Scotland.

"Standing at the head of a course in the early light of a late summer day, with the fog lifting and the sheep bleating, grass clippings sticking to the sides of your shoes and the air smelling of damp wool, the golf course is a sanctuary. You wonder, What's in store for me today? There's hope in your voice. Without hope, there is no golf."

All that is required of us to fulfil that hope is that we make the journey.

Keeper of the Greens

olf's first greenkeepers were the rabbits and sheep that roamed the landscape. It was hard to get them to work formal hours, but the hungry sheep did their best to keep the grass low enough to make possible those early fairway strokes. And as for our cute little long-eared friends, you might go as far as to say that they were unwittingly responsible for giving people the golf bug in the first place, encouraging those with the time and the inclination to have a go at knocking a stone into a rabbit's burrow, with an implement ill-designed for the purpose. And modern day golfers think the game is tough!

Still at least in medieval times, when golf was just becoming more prevalent, players had a bigger hole to aim at, for a rabbit's burrow is a considerably more inviting prospect than today's all-too-small, 4¼" affair.

The clubs used in those far off days were obviously fairly primitive, due to the limitations in materials and manufacturing processes. And to a large extent their form and function reflected the playing conditions. In the beginning, it's almost certain that the game was played with a single wooden implement, probably something resembling what we now know as a driver. But as the terrain was unkempt, this proved too limiting, so variations

▲ Sheep – golf's first greenkeepers.

▲ Old Willie Park with an early iron club. Old Willie went on to win the Open three times in the 1860s.

were then gradually introduced to cope with specific situations.

Shot making of the period also reflected the ground conditions. Unwatered linksland, even without the cultivation of human hands, was obviously a hard-running playing surface, so low bumbling shots which spent as much time on the ground as in the air tended to work best. And, as it's usually windy by the sea, a low ball flight was doubly desirable.

You could see why golfers, keen to improve the quality of their playing surface, would want to introduce some form of "gardening". But for centuries it was an incredibly disorganised business. The fact was, there weren't many golf courses, therefore there wasn't a great demand for a greenkeeper.

The golfing boom changed everything. It led to new jobs and reasonable livelihoods which had before scarcely existed. Club makers and golf ball makers thrived, as did the early

course architects. Some were ahead of the game and saw golf course design as a way to make a quick buck. One such fellow, Tom Bendelow, a Scot who migrated to America, could lay out a golf course in one day, for a fee of $25. In the late 19th and early 20th century, he perpetrated more than 600 of his creations, none of which were especially memorable. Made Tom a happy man, though. And a rich one.

Whilst most golf courses were not created with such apparent disregard for flair or detail, more and more golf courses sprung up on both sides of the Atlantic, so the demand for staff to maintain the grounds increased greatly. There was no scope for huge earth-moving endeavours and so golf courses fitted in with the landscape, a case of trying to combine a golfing challenge with a natural setting.

Old Tom Morris was probably one of the earliest known "official" keeper of the greens. He took up the post at St Andrews in 1863, commanding a grand salary of £50 per annum. He also received help from a local lad during competition weeks, when it was necessary to get the course in the best shape possible.

Then, as now, the job descriptions for any keeper of the greens extended beyond simply looking after the greens, as in putting surfaces. It included the entire golf course. And all they had in the way of tools were barrows, shovels and brushes. Typically, the men had no special knowledge of course management, either.

The keeper of the greens was, at that time, in the same boat as the architect. He could achieve, or cultivate, only what the natural terrain allowed. Mother Nature was, you might say, the early greenkeeper's boss. He just followed her lead.

But not for long. In the early 1900s greenkeeping really came into its own, for it was then that the power mower was invented. This meant that golf courses became much more cultivated and playable. Fairways could be maintained to a standard never before dreamed of. Greens were, dare one say, manicured. Imagine how golfers must have rejoiced at the smooth roll of the ball.

Meanwhile the rabbits and the sheep, the hitherto faithful four-legged agronomists, were relieved of their duties.

▲ Old and Young Tom Morris, Old Tom was the first official keeper of the greens.

The job of greenkeeper has since become a well-respected position and an ever more enticing career option. Today, greenkeeping is an art and a science. A golf course thrives and survives, literally, at the hands of one person. And that one person, in the form of a club's head greenkeeper, carries with him a great burden of responsibility. Not just to the members, but to the environment, too.

More and more, environmental considerations demand that golf courses exist in harmony with the indigenous plant and wildlife. In that sense, golf has gone full circle. We're back to where we started; building golf courses where nature is the main architect and man simply makes a few adjustments. It's not quite that simplistic, but that's the principle. And, indeed, that's what the best golf course architects want to create.

Anyone who loves the game of golf must rejoice at this development, for it is undeniably true that many of the world's best golf courses look like they were meant to be there, so perfectly do they blend in with their natural surroundings. Today's greenkeepers do a marvellous job at maintaining that image. And every living being, golfers, animals, and plant life, reaps the rewards.

▶ A greenkeeper rakes a bunker on the ninth hole before the 34th Ryder Cup at the Belfry 2002.

Links

In golf's formative years there were no golf courses, as such. It was just a case of choosing a piece of land that looked reasonably suitable for the purpose. Even up to the early part of the 18th century there was basically no such thing as a formal golf course, at least not as we know it today. At Leith near Edinburgh, for instance, golf was played over five holes measuring 414, 461, 426, 495, and 435 yards. Given the equipment of the day, these were seriously demanding holes. A round might have been three circuits of these given holes. Other courses, however, had six holes. And at Montrose, there were 25 holes.

There was no architecture or design involved; simply the natural terrain would determine the route of play. Along the stretches of coastline in Scotland where golf almost certainly

originated, this natural course would follow the relatively flat valleys which meandered between the towering dunes. That, basically, is a links golf course. Every single links course in existence today reflects these humble origins. The key strategic elements are moulded by nature.

Not that there are many links courses. In fact, less than half of one per cent of golf courses in the world are true links and much of this planet's genuine linksland has already been used up either for golf courses or human settlement. On this craggy coastal

▲ 18th century golf on links land at St Andrews.

L

▶ The ninth hole at Royal County Down.

terrain, which links the sea with the farmland, you can see how it must have so inspired the game's inventors. And it continues to be an inspiration to modern day golf course architects fortunate enough to stumble across suitable plots of land with the necessary planning consents.

Classic links design certainly didn't end while Old Tom Morris was still striding the fairways. Stunning newcomers include Kingsbarns in Fife, now a regular European Tour venue for the Dunhill Links Championship along with Carnoustie and the Old Course; Pat Ruddy's magnificent European Club, 35 miles south of Dublin; or the truly magical Greg Norman-designed Doonbeg on the west Irish coast.

Indeed, the vast majority of the world's links courses are to be found in the British Isles. And such is their pedigree and sheer class, that in *Golf World* magazine's 2002 listing of the top-100 courses in the British Isles, eight of the top-10 (and 17 of the top-23) were links layouts. Just look at this catalogue of greats. Muirfield, Royal County Down, Turnberry Ailsa, St Andrews Old Course, Royal Birkdale, Portmarnock Old Course, Royal

Portrush Dunluce, and Ballybunion Old Course. All share a wow factor of epic proportions.

Only two inland interlopers dare to share a top-10 spot with such greats; Loch Lomond and Woodhall Spa, both oozing quality in their own right. Good as they undoubtedly are, however, there is nothing – absolutely nothing – to compare with the feeling of approaching a premier links course. Some may look a little unremarkable from a distance, with only the merest sliver of fairway visible to the naked

eye, or a few distant flags bending in the wind, but once you set foot on the first tee or simply peer out from the clubhouse window, it truly captivates you. And if the weather's kind too it serves as a powerful reminder of just how lucky you are to play this game.

It is an addictive blend of natural surroundings and strategic genius. But many find that links golf can take some getting used to. The hard, uneven fairways do not always play by the rules. A pure, well-struck shot can easily get swept off in the wrong direction via

a bad bounce. But equally, a misguided stroke can get lucky and finish on the green. You hope! Because typically both fairway and greenside bunkers, are deep, cavernous and intimidating compared with those on most inland courses.

And the windswept, fast, firm putting surfaces do not always yield to the powers of modern-day equipment. Backspin can be an ineffective ally. You have to invent shots on a links that you wouldn't even entertain on an inland course; bump-and-run shots from 100 yards to help hide your ball from the ravaging effects of a seaside breeze; putting from 30 yards off the green to negotiate the humps and hollows between you and the flag. It's all part of the fun.

Tom Watson is now one of links golf's greatest advocates, but it certainly wasn't love at first sight. In his own words it wasn't until 1979 that he really began to understand and appreciate its unique nuances – by which time he'd somehow already won two of his five Open Championships! He once said that, "A great golf course both frees and challenges a player's mind". His statement encapsulates everything that is good about links golf; the aesthetics, the sheer heart-stopping impact of your surroundings as you play; and the sense of playing golf in its purest form, on an inspiring stage. No other type of course can touch a links layout for all of these qualities.

Matchplay

The term matchplay describes a match in which one golfer plays against another, or two golfers play their better ball against the better ball of two other players. That's it, in a nutshell. The actual score on each hole matters not a jot. A hole is won by the player, or pair, that takes the fewest strokes. The outcome of the match is decided when either side, or player, is "up" or "down" by more holes than there are left to play. Hence, if you are "three holes down" with only two holes left to play, you are deemed to have lost the match 3&2.

The very origins of golf are where we must look in order to unearth evidence of why matchplay was the original, most popular form of golf. The main factor was simply the variation in the number of holes on those early golf courses, which made it virtually impossible to compare strokeplay scores. So there seemed little merit in the pencil-and-card approach. Another reason to favour matchplay was the fairly haphazard attitude to the rules... there were none!

Matchplay thus established itself as the golfers' staple diet because, to all intents and purposes, it was the only viable option. The thing is, even today, many centuries on, it is the favoured format by golf's traditionalists. Such an argument carries with it considerable weight, too, for there is something

◀ Paul Casey and Jerry Kelly check their balls as their World Matchplay game hots up!

wonderful about the simplicity and raw appeal of head-to-head encounters.

Personality and character has a direct bearing on the outcome of the match, a fact which always offers added interest. The ebb and flow of the game inevitably becomes much more unpredictable. And whether you're a participant or merely a spectator, that unpredictable nature undoubtedly makes the match so much more engaging and exciting.

The drama is heightened also by the fact that, for the period of that match, there is only a pair of combatants, jostling with one another. The psychological swings are thus every bit as crucial to the outcome of the match as the quality of the golf swings on show. Every great shot executed serves to bolster the confidence of its owner and chip away at the morale of the other. Equally, every error perpetrated by one player has an uplifting effect on the spirits of the other.

This is why strokeplay, by comparison, might be considered a fairly tame affair. In a typical tournament there are as many as 150 competitors. In all truth, the behaviour or performance of one has no direct bearing on another. At least, not to the extent that is the case with matchplay and, even then, not usually until the latter stages of a tournament. The final nine is when a strokeplay tournament comes alive.

Even so, the professional game is dominated by strokeplay competition. And with good reason. A 72-hole contest is undoubtedly the fairest, and most accurate, way of determining the best player in the field on any given week. And it's not as if strokeplay competition is dull. Far from it. Golf's four major championships exist under

played in the depths of Autumn at Wentworth in Surrey but under new Volvo sponsorship is moving to the sunnier climes of Finca Cortesin Golf Club, near Malaga in Spain from 2009.

Fans love it – subject to journeymen not spoiling things and denying them the final day showdowns between the very best players such as Tiger and Padraig that they – and the TV companies – want.

But you occasionally sense the leading players aren't wholly comfortable with matchplay, sometimes over only 18 holes. It's a sprint, compared to the usual 72-hole strokeplay marathon. In a strokeplay event if Tiger Woods were to shoot a first round 68, he'd be looking forward to getting himself into contention for the weekend. Another win would perhaps be on the cards. In matchplay, he could shoot the identical score and yet his unheralded opponent could shoot one better to leave him packing his bags and heading home in his multi-million dollar private jet.

The Ryder Cup, of course, is a great spectacle for exactly this unpredictability. Add to that the interest of two great golfing powers – the

such a format and, one would have to say, these events would be considered the highlight of the year by most golfers and armchair fans.

Thankfully, though, matchplay has its place in the pro game in the shape of such events as the World Matchplay which for more than 40 years had been

United States and Europe – trying to beat the brains out of each other (with good etiquette, naturally) and you have quite a cocktail of competitive spirit to liven-up proceedings. Home and away fixtures ensure a frenzied atmosphere outside the ropes too, with the Irish finally getting their first chance to go Ryder Cup crazy in the 2006 event at the prestigious K Club in County Kildare. The Solheim Cup, initiated in 1990 by the founder of the Ping golf company, is the equivalent contest for the best women professionals.

▼ The winning 2006 Ryder Cup team at the K Club, Ireland.

The buzz and excitement of these two biennial transatlantic clashes has led to the formula being replicated elsewhere – the Presidents Cup from 1994 between the USA and Rest of the (non-European) World; the Seve Trophy from 2000 between GB&I and Continental Europe; and most recently the Royal Trophy from 2006 pitting Europe against Asia.

But that is pretty much the extent of matchplay golf in the pro game. And so it is left to amateurs in their millions to carry the torch. And how we relish it. On a weekend morning, or any morning for the lucky ones free of the constraints of a working life, there is nothing better than getting together with a group of friends and playing a friendly fourball betterball for a couple of quid. We explained the rules in an earlier chapter (see Handicap) so no need to repeat here.

But it's not just the weekend players who get to battle it out under the rules of engagement known as matchplay. It's still the format used to determine the winners of amateur golf's premier events too. In prestigious events such as the Amateur Championship, there's an initial strokeplay qualifying stage,

Suzann Pettersen of Norway and Europe holes a vital birdie putt to win the final afternoon fourball match during the 2003 Solheim Cup.

Massed crowds follow Rory McIlroy of Ireland and Billy Horschel of the USA on the ninth hole during the 2007 Walker Cup.

but after that, it's knockout matchplay singles all the way to the final. It's been like that for over 100 years. And it will be for the next 100, one hopes.

The Walker Cup, a men's team event played by the leading amateurs from the United States against those from Great Britain and Ireland, exists in broadly the same format as the Ryder Cup, with only subtle differences in the structure and running order of the days' play. The leading women amateurs have the equivalent competition in the form of the Curtis Cup, playing for a historic trophy donated in the 1930s by a pair of former US Amateur Champions from Boston, Margaret and Harriott Curtis.

Both of these events represent the pinnacle of an amateur golfer's career and many stars of the future have delayed turning professional just to be part of either of these biennial contests. That, in many ways, sums up the extent to which matchplay golf appeals to all golfers. Long may we all be held in its grip.

Nicklaus

Let's get one thing straight... for the record... just in case, heaven forbid, there's any confusion out there. Jack Nicklaus is the greatest golfer who ever lived. I repeat, Jack Nicklaus is the greatest. It's not a difficult one to grasp. In fact, it's a total no-brainer.

Before you go shouting "in the name of Tiger Woods, what is the man talking about?", just allow me to put forward a compelling case over the next 900 or so words.

If we take the story back to the early days, not surprisingly we learn that young Jack made phenomenal progress from the moment he first picked up a golf club. He was a natural athlete and excelled in many sports at school. But once he found golf, and then learned he had a serious gift for the game, it consumed him. By the age of 13 he was Ohio State Junior champion and

his handicap was down to plus-3! Soon he was regularly shooting 64s and 63s, bagging junior and state championships with ridiculous ease.

The pro game beckoned, but not before he'd won the US Amateur Championship twice. Now he could really get into his stride. In his first year as a tour pro, 1962, his maiden victory was the US Open – an emphatic statement of intent, making him the first

man since Bobby Jones to hold the US Amateur and US Open titles simultaneously.

That his first tournament win was a major was a sign of things to come, for it was golf's big four events that Jack loved most. He won tournaments all over the world. Indeed, in 1971, arguably playing the best golf of his life, he won three tournaments in a row by margins of eight, eight, and seven shots. Jack was capable of incredible bursts of scoring.

But the majors were Jack's focus and he geared his entire playing schedule around them. He wanted to reach peak form during those crucial four weeks and somehow managed to achieve that goal more than anyone in the history of the game. His incredible record in the majors has been recounted many times, but can never be told too often.

Within four years of turning pro, he'd managed to win the Grand Slam.

By 1971, only nine years after turning pro, he'd become the first man to win all four majors at least twice. And seven years later, he'd won each of them at least three times. When he won his final major championship, the 1986 Masters, his tally had risen to 18.

And just take a look at the consistency of the man. In the Masters between 1963 and 1977 his run of finishes looks like this: Won, 2nd, Won,

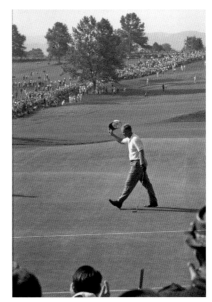

◄◄ Jack Nicklaus playing the Masters as an amateur in 1961.

◄ Jack wins his first tournament as a pro – the 1962 US Open.

Won, MC, 5th, 24th, 8th, 2nd, Won, 3rd, 4th, Won, 3rd, 2nd! In the Open Championship during the same period, and including 1978, it looks like this: 3rd, 2nd, 12th, Won, 2nd, 2nd, 6th, Won, 5th, 2nd, 4th, 3rd, 3rd, 2nd, 2nd, Won! It's simply extraordinary.

Some argue that Jack didn't have to compete against the same quality of opposition that exists at the top of the game today. Well, there may not quite have been the same strength in depth but can anyone seriously suggest that Jack didn't have anyone decent to beat? How about Arnold Palmer, Gary Player, Johnny Miller, Tom Watson, Lee Trevino and Tom Weiskopf? And that's just for starters.

In his prime, Jack knew he was the best. Not that he'd ever say as much. But then again, he didn't need to. His opponents knew Jack was the best, too. Jack had that one quality which separates the great from the good; a champion's temperament. That meant that if ever his golf game let him down, his head would get him out of trouble. So if he played well, he'd win. And if he played indifferently, he'd still win, because he was the smartest. He managed his game that well. He was so

◄◄ Jack celebrates winning the 1966 Open at Muirfield, thus completing golf's Grand Slam.

◄ Arnold Palmer helping Jack into his 1963 Masters jacket.

cool, so calm and so composed that he made few really costly mistakes under the most intense pressure, while others around him simply wilted in the heat.

You have to trust the judgement of the people who know best. Like Arnold Palmer who, when asked who was the greatest commented, "I think Nicklaus would have to be given that nod". Or his other great friend and rival Gary Player who simply says, "The greatest scorer who ever lived was Jack Nicklaus".

Tiger Woods, with 14 majors by the end of 2008, is of course the other name most mentioned in any debate about who is the greatest. And his is, indeed, a strong case. Sure, he has shot lower scores than Jack in majors. He's often won by bigger margins, too. Yes, in certain bursts of play he is probably a better golfer than Jack.

But look at Jack's longevity. His major victories span 24 years, the 1962

US Open to the 1986 Masters. Look not at just the 18 major championships to his name, or that he won every major at least three times, but to the fact that he also registered another 46 second and third place finishes in majors and a total of 73 top-10s.

Fittingly, Jack's love affair with our Open Championship, and indeed his competitive playing career, came to an end at St Andrews in 2005 after 38 appearances spanning five decades – second only to Gary Player. Jack missed the halfway cut by two strokes, but did roll home a 12-foot putt amid raucous cheering on the 18th on Friday to ensure things came to an end with a birdie. Entirely appropriate.

The Royal Bank of Scotland chose the occasion to launch a Jack Nicklaus commemorative five pound note, thus making him only the third living person to feature on a Scottish bank note apart from The Queen and her late mother.

Only when Tiger nears the end of his playing career can we truly compare the records. Only then can Tiger lay claim to the greatest golfer tag. Until that point, Nicklaus is ahead...on points.

But, as Tiger might say, the fight goes on.

Old Course

Almost anyone with even a remotely passing interest in the game is aware that St Andrews is the home of golf. There are records to suggest that golf has been played for more than 450 years on the patch of land which is now known as the Old Course, which is mind-boggling when you think about it.

Everything about the game of golf as we know it originates from this ancient Scottish town. Inside the grey stone walls of the splendid Royal & Ancient clubhouse, which was built in

◀◀ Jack Nicklaus hits his tee shot on the 18th hole at his last British Open.

◀ St Andrews Old Course hosting a match in 1903.

▼ Tiger Woods on his way to winning in 2005.

1754 and stands prominently behind the 18th green and first tee, resides golf's ruling body, overseeing the well-being of the game throughout the world, except the United States and Mexico. Back in 1763, the R&A members would have witnessed the single most fundamental change in the history of the Old Course, when it was changed from the original 22 holes to something resembling today's 18.

Since then, it has played host to the Open Championship, the oldest and greatest tournament in the world, no less than 27 times and is due to host it again in 2010. It has been tweaked and extended over the years reaching 7,279 yards for 2005's event, with "Long", the aptly named 14th hole stretching to 618 yards – the longest in Open Championship history. And long hitters have fared well round the venerable course of late with John Daly winning in 1995 and Tiger Woods' two Open victories coming here in 2000 and 2005.

But the essence of what makes the Old Course special remains gloriously intact. On a windy day, it remains the toughest of tests – even for today's players with their high-tech, computer-designed golf clubs. Part of the reason for this is that many of its hazards, which are scattered and frequently hidden, are among the most legendary, fearsome and dangerous in golf.

Hell Bunker needs no explanation, only that it should be avoided at all costs. The Swilcan Burn, which meanders across the first and 18th fairways, used to be a natural, sandy-edged water hazard. In the 1800s it was even used by local women to wash their

◀ One of golf's finest, Bobby Jones, tees off the first hole in 1927.

clothes, which were then laid out on the fairway and surrounding bushes to dry. It became such a hazard that the R&A introduced local rules specifically to outline the relief procedures in the event that your ball was caught up in the washing.

Nowadays it is a well-defined hazard, perilous enough without the added obstruction once provided by the washing. It may not often catch out the world's best players during Open Championship week, but it's the ruin of many expectant golfers'

first hole aspirations. Never mind. It's such a historic spot. Indeed, the walk across the famous Swilcan Bridge (originally the route into this ancient city from the west) is probably, no definitely, the most photographed location in world golf.

The Valley of Sin is another dastardly trap for thousands of golfers. The good, the great, and the plain average have come to grief in this hollow at the front of the 18th green. And each has Old Tom Morris to thank, for it was he who redesigned the final green at the

▲ The famous 17th with its infamous bunker.

end of the 19th century, when he was performing the dual role of greenkeeper and club professional. Visually, the Valley of Sin looks rather benign compared to some of St Andrews' more fearsome hazards, but from its sunken hollow it really is the devil's own job trying to judge the speed of a putt.

There are other wonderfully quirky features. The fourth hole is known as "Ginger Beer" because that's the spot where for many years an old local woman sold her brew to passing golfers. Granny Clark's Wynd, the road which runs across the first and 18th fairways, is named after a local fisherwoman. There is even a pair of humps in front of the 15th green bearing the colourful name, Miss Grainger's Bosoms. How inviting!

Not everyone immediately falls for the charms of St Andrews Old Course, though. It's no secret that Bobby Jones tore up his scorecard the first time he played here, after failing to escape from the deep bunker at the front of the 11th green. But he grew to love the place and rated his time at St Andrews above everything else he achieved and experienced in the game of golf. The highest of praise.

The first-time visitor might easily be fooled, as Jones was, into thinking that St Andrews might be...whisper it, overrated. Because at first sight, the Old Course can indeed look quite bleak and not at all appealing. Even as you venture out on the early holes, you might wonder what all the fuss is about. But, as Jones discovered, this is a golf course which you learn to love. And it's hard not to.

It is located on a very narrow strip of land on the Eden estuary, which largely lends the layout its most distinguishing characteristics. Anywhere to the left off the tee tends to be safe, if you can stay out of one of the many evil little bunkers, but it does make your approach shot into the greens that much tougher.

Many of the holes share huge double greens. In fact, there are seven in total, and it's quite possible, given a crooked enough approach shot, to have a putt of something like 100 yards. Yes, 100 yards! In one Open Championship, American Mark Calcavecchia was so flummoxed by this challenge that he took out his sand-wedge and pitched his ball towards the hole, in the process taking a divot out of the pristine putting surface – a deed which earned him boos from the locals in the gallery. The slopes on and around some of the greens might lead you to believe that the greenkeeper has buried some elephants under there.

It is utterly unique. And even if you aren't a huge fan of the course's aesthetics, you cannot fail to be in awe of the history which oozes from every hump, hollow, bunker, tee and green. You are literally walking in the footsteps of every golfing great who ever lived. The Old Course is magical and rightly still regarded as the Mecca of golf. Don't dilly-dally, then. Make the pilgrimage as soon as, and as often as, you possibly can.

P

Putting

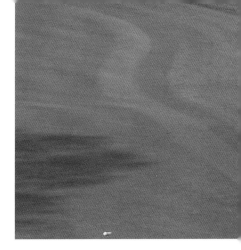

Putting is often referred to as the "game within a game", an innocuous statement which doesn't come close to summing up the degrees of torture which golfers through the generations have experienced in this discipline. Rolling a ball a few paces across what appears to be a very smooth surface seems so... well, easy. Yet somehow, it just isn't. In fact, it's so the opposite of easy that it ceased to be funny... about three centuries ago.

Not for the first time, that wise golfing guru John Jacobs hit the nail on the head when he described the vagaries of putting in his best selling book *Practical Golf*. Jacobs wrote, "How good you are at hitting the ball through the air bears little relation to how well you can roll it along the ground. The old lady at the seaside playing to amuse her grandchild can be better at it than the world class professional, playing for a fortune."

And that's the nub of it. That's what makes it so maddening. You can be the best ball-striker in the world, launching arrow-straight drives 300 yards down the middle of the fairway and striking your irons sweeter than Claudia Schiffer wrapped in candy floss. But when asked to coax the ball into a 4¼" hole, the knees go weak, the hands tremble, and the brain turns to mush. The shortest stroke in golf proves to be the toughest. It makes you want to cry.

Dave Pelz, the former NASA scientist who has made a handsome living out of studying and teaching the short game, concludes that roughly 45 per cent of shots played in a typical

round are putts for both amateurs and professionals. Your best scores usually come when your putt percentage dips below this – when the hole looks as big as a bucket; you see the line clearly; you hole a few medium-to-long putts and don't miss any tiddlers. On days like that, you wonder what all the fuss is about.

Next day, it's gone! Completely and utterly disappeared. You feel you're doing the same thing, but you putt like a blind man. And searching for the solution can be like grasping at thin air.

Perhaps one thing that makes putting such an enduring mystery is that there is no single, correct way to putt. These days anything seems to go in terms of putting technique – and

putter design. Broomhandle or belly putters anchored against chin, chest or midriff have proved lifesavers for many top pros. Others have found new ways to hold conventional length putters – left hand below right, the "clamp" style employed successfully by Bernhard Langer for a while, and perhaps most famously, top American, Chris DiMarco's ungainly "claw" grip also dubbed the "psycho" grip by his bemused, and perhaps slightly envious PGA Tour chums. Anything that works really.

The runaway success of the Odyssey 2-Ball putter has also sparked a new wave of futuristic designs, many of which wouldn't look out of place on

◀ It happens to the best. Craig Stadler misses a tiny putt on the 18th green at the 1985 Ryder Cup.

▼ Sam Torrance using his broomhandle putter at the 1994 Masters.

1.

though certainly not all as seen above – adhere to certain key principles, which are generally considered good for your putting. There are no musts, but if you're struggling on the greens, this could help:

1. Try gripping the club so your hands are parallel to the putter-face – in other words, the palms face one another, each square to the target. This will encourage the hands to work in harmony with one another, rather than independently which can upset the path of the stroke.

2. Establish a posture whereby your eyes are directly over, or slightly behind, the ball. This helps you see the line more clearly at address.

These two factors are common to many of the world's great putters, as is the correct mental attitude. This is where the biggest difference lies between poor and accomplished putters. The former tend to approach the green with a sense of dread, or at the very least trepidation, because they doubt their ability. It becomes a self-fulfilling prophecy. As Lee Trevino once said, "If you start to tell yourself that you can't putt, you can bet your bottom peso that you won't be able to get it in the hole from three feet". Quite!

the set of *Star Wars*. Titleist's Scotty Cameron Futura is one of the most unconventional, while the heads on Ping's Doc 17 and Odyssey's Tri-Ball are now the size of tea plates.

So when we look to the golfing greats for inspiration, we see that they all putt differently using a wide variety of putter styles. The only shared characteristic is that they hole a lot of putts. But how? Well, the majority –

Easier said than done, but not impossible if we practise. Partly it comes down to a change in outlook. Club golfers putt very defensively, almost to not miss rather than hole it. It leads to indecisiveness. We tend to drag it, steer it, jab at it, anything but stroke it confidently towards the hole.

Even the pros suffer from this. Brad Faxon, who putts like an angel, was once seen randomly hitting putts off the end of the putting green one after another, with no apparent target in mind. When another player, curious as to the purpose of such a drill, asked what he was doing, Faxon replied, "I'm practising not caring". He was just trying to introduce the feeling you have when you're playing golf as a kid. You just look, aim, and hit. Ironically, with not even the slightest consideration for the consequences of missing you tend to hole out more often.

Leading sports psychologist, Dr Bob Rotella, says the secret is learning to love putting. "Oh good, now we get to putt. This is where I come to life. This is where I can express my imagination and artistry; this is where I can kick some butt!" That's the attitude he thinks we need to cultivate.

It's a classic sporting conundrum, which only the very best seem able to cope with especially under pressure – you need to putt like you don't care, when in fact you do as it brings freedom to your stroke, leading to a better strike and smoother roll.

No wonder putting drives us mad!

Quadrilateral

When Bobby Jones incredibly won the British Amateur Championship, the Open Championship, the US Open and the US Amateur Championship in the same calendar year, 1930, it rendered even the most hardened golf journalist lost for words. Then one day a New York based writer called Jones' achievement "The Impregnable Quadrilateral". The title stuck.

Seventy-odd years later, Jones' feat that year still takes some believing. He was 28 years of age, at the peak of his powers, and he wasn't even playing for money. Imagine what this extraordinary amateur might have achieved if the added motivation of money had been thrown into the mix?

Actually, it wouldn't have made a scrap of difference, because Jones was born into a wealthy Atlanta family and

had never known what it was like to have money troubles. And besides, he loved the game for all its purest virtues and therefore cash was never of any consequence, the professional game never a temptation.

Maybe that explains why Jones retired from competitive golf at the end of his triumphant 1930 season. He had achieved all that was of interest to him, won all the tournaments that mattered.

career than one glorious season, though. The man did, after all, win a total of four US Opens (he was also runner–up another three times), a single Amateur Championship and five US Amateur Championships. It's fair to say he dominated the world of golf for the best part of 10 years. And the impression he left on these shores when he came over to Britain to compete in the Open Championship, which he went on to win three times, was just as emphatic.

Jones' first ever visit to Britain was surprisingly unsuccessful. He entered the Amateur Championship in 1921, but lost in the fourth round, then playing later that summer in the Open

Bobby Jones with the Open trophy, US Open trophy, US Amateur trophy and the Walker Cup.

Jones at the 1921 British Amateur Championship, Hoylake.

It was time to move on. He could, and did, continue to play golf for fun in between his business practising law and creating the most beautiful golf course in the history of the game, Augusta National.

There has never been, and in truth there probably never will be, another more sublime illustration of a sports person quitting while they were ahead.

There was more to Jones' playing

▲ Bobby Jones on his way to winning the 1926 Open at Royal Lytham & St Annes.

Championship at St Andrews, petulantly tore up his card in the third round. It was an uncharacteristic lapse in etiquette from a man who became synonymous with all that was good about the game of golf.

Five years after that first visit, Jones returned to compete in the 1926 Open Championship at Royal Lytham & St Annes on the rugged Lancashire coastline. He brought with him a reputation for fine iron play, beautiful putting, and consistent scoring. All of these powers were much in evidence as he opened with a pair of fine 72s. Over the course of the final two rounds Jones' calm, level-headed temperament and astute course management saw him home by a couple of shots from fellow American Al Watrous. Jones had won his first Open.

The following year at St Andrews, there was to be no such close contest. Jones spread-eagled the field like never before in championship history. Several golfers accumulated four-round totals which would have won the Open in previous years, but none were even within touching distance of the masterful Jones.

His opening round of 68 was exceptional even by his high standards. He added to that scores of 72, 73 and 72 to win by six shots. When he holed his final putt on the 18th green, the crowd rushed towards him and carried him shoulder high off the golf course, his elevated frame subjected to a barrage of congratulatory pats on the back! Having torn up his card at his last visit to St Andrews, he left this time a conquering hero.

The colourful character Walter Hagen won the next two Opens, reinforcing the American stranglehold on the Claret Jug, but Jones got to complete his hat-trick when the championship returned to Hoylake in 1930. Here again Jones came and conquered, setting records along the way. Indeed, his winning total was 10 strokes lower than Walter Hagen's winning score the last time the championship was played at Hoylake, only six years previously.

This was the year, of course, when Jones was virtually unbeatable. He'd already won the US Open and the Amateur Championship by the time he arrived at Hoylake. And after he left Jones went on to win the US Amateur Championship, thereby completing the final leg of his famous quadrilateral.

It was such a shame for golf that Jones chose to retire, for he left a void. Fans on both sides of the Atlantic would seldom again be able to witness that swing of metronome-like rhythm and exquisitely timed ball striking, or the pure swing of his famous Calamity Jane putter, which he wielded to such devastating effect.

▼ Jones with the 1926 Open trophy.

In recompense, Jones gave so much back to the game. Of course, he was the founder of the tournament which became golf's fourth major championship, the Masters, when he initiated an exclusive invitational tournament at Augusta National. He wrote astutely on the techniques of the game. And his gentlemanly conduct and gracious behaviour on and off the golf course, became an inspiration to all others who aspired and dreamed to follow in his footsteps.

So sad, then, that Jones should suffer the fate of a terrible debilitating illness which later in life confined him to a wheelchair. No one, of course, deserves such a fate and yet somehow it seems more tragic when a great athlete such as Jones is so physically stricken. He eventually died at the age of 69.

His legacy is a fitting tribute to the man's qualities both on and off the field of play; a beautiful golf course and a championship that lives on in his memory, and the most extraordinary passage of play in the history of golf. For be in no doubt about this fact; Jones' quadrilateral will never again be repeated.

THE A TO Z OF GOLF

Rules of Golf

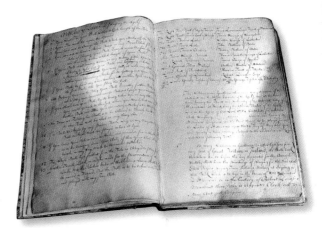

Pity the poor old Rules of Golf. Dull and unloved by the masses, they just want to be seen to do the right thing. But no one seems to appreciate them. Talk about left on the shelf. That's the fate of most rules books.

Trouble is, they appear so complex. Those who do summon up the motivation to delve into their pages bore themselves half to death with the sheer volume of tedious jargon and endless subparagraphs and appendices. Those few who find the subject strangely absorbing usually become rules officials, a cruel fate in itself.

Of course, it never used to be like this. In the long distant past, life was so much simpler. And so were the rules of golf. It was a group called the Royal Company of Edinburgh Golfers, officially recognised as the oldest golf club in the world, who in 1744 first got together and decided the game needed a set of regulations to ensure everyone played fair and square. Up to that point, there were no rules – except, as Mary Queen of Scots might have said, "don't lose your head". Golf was a relatively happy-go-lucky affair.

But the Royal Company rightly felt this oversight was plainly ridiculous. So they seized the initiative. And one can only imagine the buzz of excitement which filled the room that day as they discussed the new regulations which

would effectively govern the way the game was played. And do you know something? They could think of only 13 rules. Yes, 13. That's all.

Essentially these first 13 rules were fairly rudimentary codes of conduct, most of which might be considered a little bizarre by today's standards. For example, the player on the green who was farthest away from the hole would putt first. They had to. There was no choice in the matter and none of the niceties that we see today, such as marking the ball closest to the hole, or tapping-in as a courtesy to "get out of the way" of the other players about to putt.

Nope. If your playing partner, or opponent, putted up to within a few inches of the hole and their ball happened to come to rest in such a way as to block your route to the hole, it was tough luck. You had to find a way past it. You would frequently see golfers chipping from two or three feet away, to effectively "hurdle" over an opponent's ball, which was ludicrous. That rule was known as the "stymie" and, of course, it became an integral part of the matchplayer's art – a bit like laying a snooker, really. In 1952

◄◄ Harry Vardon negotiating a stymie in 1903.

◄ The rules allow you to play out of the St Andrews' burn, but as Mr Neville will vouch from May 1923, it is sometimes best to take a drop.

it was abolished as being an "unfair advantage" and an "embarrassment". In all truth, it was surprising that this rule took as long to ban as it did. Still, better late than never.

By the mid-19th century, the golfing bodies felt the need to expand the rule book to accommodate some scenarios that were evidently a regular occurrence on the golf course, yet which had no official rule to dictate the correct procedure. So the Royal and Ancient Golf Club of St Andrews, who to this day jointly assume responsibility for the running of the game with the USGA, extended the original 13 rules to 22. That version soon became universally accepted as the official *Rules of Golf.*

Of course, the rules have since evolved, mushroomed, spiralled out of control, or become a vast tome of desert-dry text – depending on your viewpoint. They are actually revised every four years when a potentially long agenda is whittled down by the appropriate committee to just a few rules that need tweaking, rewording or rethinking to stay abreast of trends and changes in the game.

Much recent regulation concerns equipment as the guardians of the game seek to ensure its challenge is not diminished by technology's relentless march. So drivers can only be so big, so long and impart so much energy to the ball. Some view this as essential; others as trying to hold back the tide Canute-style – either way equipment regulation is definitely the rulemakers' biggest headache right now.

Some traditionalists say that golf actually only needs one rule; you play the ball as it lies and do not touch it from the moment you place it on the tee to the time you bend down and pick it out of the cup. At first, this appears workable, but the argument sadly doesn't bear close scrutiny, certainly not in the professional game.

And so the rule book now extends to over 100 pages and boasts an even more comprehensive 500-page sister publication with the snappy, award-winning title, *Decisions on the Rules of Golf.* This reveals in minute detail what you should do if, for instance, a crawfish mound interferes with your stance or swing. Seriously, it's in there!

In amongst the weird and the wonderful, the essence of the original

13 rules remains, though it's safe to say those pioneering rule makers might be a little bewildered by the 21st century version – just like the majority of club golfers, in fact!

But any golfer with a love for the game would be justifiably concerned if the rules were not so rigidly, and extensively, applied. Golf is the only truly self-governing sport. As such, every participant has an obligation to try to be aware of and abide by the rules, many of which require only a modicum of common sense to help you interpret the correct procedures for the vast majority of on-course eventualities.

Only when the occasional googly gets thrown our way do we have to delve into the pages of the rule book. So it's prudent for at least one of your playing group to have a copy tucked in their golf bag. Chances are it won't be needed very often but you never know – better safe than sorry.

◀ It's not that often that a rulebook is needed but here's a case in point.

Slice

There are no official figures on the number of golfers in the world who suffer from a slice. They don't yet put that kind of information on the census, although given the ludicrous notion that you can legitimately state your religion as "Vulcan" maybe the section headed "chosen shot persuasion" isn't so far-fetched.

Still, we digress. The fact is, probably three-quarters of the world's golfers are afflicted by a slice, a power-sapping shot which causes the ball to fly on a weak trajectory from left-to-right through the air. As if you didn't know! You've been staring at the hateful creation all your golfing life, probably.

As we gave you a cure for five other common ailments earlier in the book (see Faults and Fixes) it would be cruel to not offer the same treatment for slicers, who as we say are among the

vast majority at club level. So here we go; the reasons why you slice and how you can eliminate it from your game. The advice which follows applies to the longest clubs in the bag, specifically the driver, as these straight-faced clubs are the ones most prone to an attack of the wicked slice.

First things first; let's analyse the actual geometry of the slice, because this information will help accelerate the correction process. The path of the swing is out-to-in, which means the clubhead is travelling to the left

of the target at impact, or across the line. The clubface is also open to that path, so you get a glancing blow which creates clockwise spin on the ball. The ball starts to the left, which reflects the path of the clubhead, then swerves to the right in the air, which reflects the sidespin on the ball generated by the open clubface. That's it, in a nutshell.

So how do these faulty impact factors come about? What's the root cause? Well, it starts at the address position. More often than not, the ball is too far forward in the stance. In other words, too

far to the left relative to where your feet are. That has a negative chain reaction, in as much that you have to reach for the ball which drags your shoulders into a position whereby they align left of the target. Standing in that fashion, it's impossible to do anything but swing on an out-to-in path. This is a key point of understanding in the geometry of your golf shots; the path of your swing is pre-determined by the ball position.

Of course, swinging to the left means the ball flies to the left, so as an instinctive reaction to counteract that

▶ The slice cure starts with a good set up.

▶ ...which then promotes a good on-line takeaway.

you open the clubface and effectively "slice" the ball back into play. It's a little bit like a backhand slice in tennis. There's no release. And as a result, there's no power.

So the way to correct a slice is to go back to the start of the problem, your address position, and systematically rectify the individual faults. Make sure the ball is placed opposite your left heel; absolutely and definitely no further forward than that. This immediately squares-up your shoulders, so they are aligned parallel with the ball-to-target line.

Remember, the path of your swing is pre-determined by your ball position. So what you'll find is that it will feel easier, natural even, to swing the club on the correct path. The clubhead approaches the ball from inside, not outside, the line. It then reaches the on-line portion of its arc at the exact moment of impact, so the ball starts on-line. Your first few shots may slice to the right in the air, as you'll still be keeping the clubface open as if you were playing for a slice. But instinctively you'll start to square the clubface to produce a straight shot.

Think in terms of a topspin forehand in tennis, the right hand rolling over through the ball. That release action produces much more power and something you might not have seen before; a proper draw flight. You'll enjoy that. As you will the extra distance that comes with that kind of strike and trajectory. In fact, you could reasonably expect to gain another 15-20 per cent in terms of the yardage of your best drives. And it will feel easy, it really will.

Another benefit of curing your slice is that you have less of a tendency to pull your shots, a fault which is very closely related to the slice. The pull shares the slice's out-to-in swing path, the difference being that the clubface stays square to the path of the swing, rather than open as is the case with the slice. It's more prevalent among the lofted clubs, where the extra backspin basically cancels out the sidespin.

As with the advice we offered on the driver, just make sure the ball isn't too far forward with your iron shots, as that has the effect of opening your shoulder alignment to the left. And, as we now know, that causes you to swing to the left. Get that ball position spot-on, for good shoulder alignment, and you'll swing more on-line and hit straight, solid iron shots.

◀ ...a good top of backswing position.

◀ ...and ideal impact, with ball starting on line.

Tiger

There are only three player's names that make it into this alphabetical expedition through golf. The first, Bobby Jones, is a legend. The second, Jack Nicklaus, almost indisputably holds the title of greatest player in history. And the third, Tiger Woods, is the only realistic living threat to that crown.

If you have a spare seven or eight hours you could read his entire biography on the PGA Tour's website! Most significantly, he's already won 14 major championships, which is very impressive going. He still has some way to go as Big Jack won 18. But Tiger has only just turned 30 and has time on his side, assuming he stays fit and healthy and, crucially, manages to maintain his desire.

Despite knee surgery in the 2002 and 2008 seasons, his fitness appears intact. Given the extraordinary physical demands of his swing, it is foolhardy to expect Tiger to remain totally injury-free throughout his career. But he has a phenomenal physique, more akin to a middleweight boxer than a golfer, which will help keep serious ailments at bay.

As for desire, there's no question Tiger's ambition stems not from the dollar, but from the pure instinct born of a competitive nature. A recent knee injury in 2008 gave him an excuse to call time on his career and although he missed several Majors and a Ryder Cup victory there was no doubting that he would return, driven on by the yearning to beat Jack Nicklaus' record of 18 Major triumphs and the basic will to win. Let's face it, if he was in the game for money, he would have retired years ago with enough cash in the bank to last him several lifetimes.

It was on December 30th 1975, in Cypress California, that this star was born. If we're to believe Tiger's father, Tiger had changed his grip from two-handed to Vardon while still in his cot and before he could walk had learnt how to hit a fade using his rattle and dummy. Well, maybe not quite, but by the time he was five he'd shot his first

59...on a 9-hole pitch and putt, mind. At six, he'd played a televised exhibition match against Sam Snead. And at eight, he'd broken 80 for 18 holes on a proper grown-up golf course.

When he started playing seriously in the amateur ranks it was ridiculous. Tiger won three US Junior Amateur titles in a row and then a hat-trick of US Amateur titles too – something not even the great Bobby Jones achieved.

When he turned pro in September 1996, some bookmakers quoted odds of 33-1 for him to make the following year's Ryder Cup team. By the spring of the following year, having played in only a dozen or so PGA Tour

Tiger celebrates winning his third consecutive US Amateur trophy in 1996.

Celebrating again after yet another birdie.

▲ Tiger looks anxiously after his drive during the third round of the 1997 Masters. He needn't have worried.

in Masters history, and only one shy of the all-time major record set by Old Tom Morris in the 1862 Open Championship.

He soon had that record too! At the 2000 US Open at Pebble Beach Tiger surpassed even his own extraordinary standards in winning by 15 shots. He was 12-under par – the runner-up three over. The following month he won the Open Championship at St Andrews by eight shots, incredibly not once visiting one of the Old Course's hundred or so bunkers. It was the ultimate display of controlled power allied to precision and patience. Soon afterwards *Golf World* magazine featured a picture of Tiger on the cover with the headline "Greetings Earthlings!"

events, he was top of the US points qualification list! He'd already won six times by then, including the most astonishing performance in Masters history.

During that unforgettable week at Augusta, records fell like ninepins. Tiger beat the lowest four round total, held equally by Jack Nicklaus and Ray Floyd. He was the most under par for the treacherous back nine, 16-under. He had the lowest ever middle 36 holes (131) and the largest ever 54-hole lead, nine shots. His eventual 12-stroke victory was the biggest winning margin

Since that period, when at one point he held all four major championship trophies – a Grand Slam of sorts – Tiger has not always been quite so invincible. Others like Ernie Els, Phil Mickelson and Vijay Singh have raised their games to compete with him, and at times Tiger has just not played as well as he did throughout 2000. But that doesn't mean he's ever been in a slump. The mere suggestion is plainly ridiculous. Unless you describe winning six tournaments in the space of 10 months, as Tiger did in 2003, a slump. Okay, 2004 was tame by his standards with just two wins – one of which was in Japan. But he still finished 4th on the PGA Tour Money List, and then came back in style in 2005 to triumph by over $2.5 million from Vijay Singh after scooping six victories and a hatful of top 10s.

The fact is every great golfer goes through "flat" periods. During the late 1960s and early 1970s even Jack Nicklaus went 12 majors, or three years, without a win. Didn't stop him winning four of the next eight! Tiger went majorless too in 2003 and 2004 but struck back with the Masters and the Open in 2005, and more recently the US Open in 2008 to keep him right on track for Jack's record. That's the thing about the truly great champions. They don't just suddenly lose it. They have something extra, which allows them to find a way to win.

Of course, Tiger will have periods when he isn't dominant and isn't winning major championships right, left and centre. But he probably has another 10 years of great golf left in him before you could say he's even close to his sell-by date. So theoretically, he could play in at least another 40 major championships.

On that basis he needs a "one in ten" strike rate to equal Jack. So he can still afford the odd majorless year! Before Tiger, it seemed an impossible task. You just figured Jack's name would sit on top of the majors list for eternity. It's going to be a tough call with his suspect knee and other players raising their games, but with Tiger's burning desire to be the best ever, more and more people are beginning to feel that he could just do it.

If Tiger does beat Jack's record, then it's hard to envisage there will be a greater sporting achievement this century.

▼ Tiger Woods and Rocco Mediate who he beat at the 2008 US Open.

Tiger Woods and Rocco Mediate who he beat at the 2008 US Open.

Ungainly

The golf swing is the signature of the player. That being the case, there is some pretty strange handwriting out there on tour. With golf though, more than any other sport, you have to give credence to the old adage that "it isn't how, but how many". For unlikely as it may seem, an ungainly golf swing can also be a winning golf swing. The history of championship golf has told us as much.

Actually, in the 21st century we're a little bereft of truly ungainly swingers. If there was a club, there could be only one honorary member; America's Jim Furyk, a fine player and the 2003 US Open champion. Man, what a golf swing! He takes the club back very much in a straight line, gets slightly outside the line at the top and in an upright position, which suggests he was once fearful of the drawbacks of an overly flat swing. He then re-routes the club to the inside with an exaggerated drive of the legs and clearing of the left side, which allows free passage for the hands and arms to swing through to his trademark high-hands finish.

Words can't really do it justice, for it is an extraordinary thing to behold. You'd be wise not to copy it, but the thing is he's one of the most consistent golfers on the PGA

Tour, a man who has amassed dozens of top-10 finishes. "Go figure", as they say in Jim's homeland.

John Daly's swing is a fairly amazing piece of work, too. Conventional wisdom suggests the club should stop close to parallel, or level with the ground, at the top of the backswing. But if you were to stand opposite John you'd see that at the top of his backswing the club points down at five o'clock. It is the biggest over-swing in the history of successful golfers. It works for John, but anyone thinking about copying it had better know a very good chiropractor.

As we said, though, weird swings are few and far between. That's not to say that all of the world's top-50 players could be described as classic swingers in the mould of, say, an Ernie Els. But nearly all could be categorised as conventional, bordering on the correct. And if you look at the breed of young, up-and-coming players, it's even more noticeably the case.

There are many reasons for this, primarily that the general standard of coaching has improved out of all recognition in the last 20 or 30 years, and also that young golfers now have far greater access to this coaching. The wannabe stars of the future tend to develop very correct golf swings when they're growing up, simply refining their methods as they work their way up the golfing ladder.

So golf has become more conventional, in the technical sense. But that doesn't stop us going back through the years to a time when conventional wasn't quite so cool and weird swingers walked the earth, scaring small children and keeping the adult viewers amused at the same time.

Likeable Irishman Eamonn Darcy's swing was perhaps the benchmark for

◀ Jim Furyk and his ungainly swing on their way to winning the 2003 US Open.

▼ Big John Daly gets ready to unleash another monstrous drive.

weirdness, which sounds cruel but isn't meant to be. He'd be the first to admit that his golf swing was no thing of beauty. Indeed, it was once memorably described by one commentator as resembling "an octopus falling out of a tree". It's unlikely Darcy took offence, for what did he care? He made millions swinging his own sweet, albeit weird, way. He played Ryder Cup golf; why, he even holed the winning putt for the Europeans in the 1987 match at Muirfield Village in Ohio. The man

could play a bit!

So could Lee Trevino. In his prime, Trevino was regarded by many as being the greatest ball striker and shot maker in the game. He had what you might call an ungainly swing. He addressed the ball with a wide, slightly open stance. He then took the club back outside the line and re-routed it, figure-of-eight fashion, on to the ideal path approaching impact. He did it so successfully, in fact, that no one else kept the clubface square, travelling on-line, for longer. It placed huge strain on his lower back, but it sure did help him hit a lot of quality golf shots.

Going back even further there was Walter Hagen, a flamboyant character with a golf swing which reflected his first love, baseball. He had a big wide stance and there was a tremendous amount of lateral movement, swaying off the ball in the backswing and then lunging quite dramatically towards the target as he delivered each significant blow. It certainly lacked beauty, but it got the job done... and then some. Hagen was the greatest matchplay golfer who ever lived and his tally of 11 major championships, compiled in an era when there were only three (the Masters didn't exist when Hagen was in his prime) is second only to Jack Nicklaus.

So there have been a lot of strange, winning golf swings, over the years. And while aesthetically you'd say they had nothing in common, each did in fact have a single shared characteristic; a fine impact position. At the moment of truth, when the clubface met the ball, the key impact factors essential to good ball striking were present – namely, good swing path, correct angle of attack, a square clubface, and plenty of clubhead speed. The golf ball won't ever argue with the laws of physics. It couldn't care less what the swing looks like.

We should probably conclude with the wise words of John Jacobs, who has repeated on many occasions the phrase, "The only purpose of the golf swing is to move the club through the ball, square to the target, at maximum speed. How this is done is of no significance at all, so long as the method employed enables it to be done repetitively". Exactly.

◀ Eamonn Darcy knocks one up the middle at the Qatar Masters in his inimitable style.

▼ Walter Hagen lunges at another, this time at Troon in the 1923 Open.

Veterans

► Lee Trevino, still joking at the 2004 Toshiba Senior Masters.

In the realms of professional sport it's hard to think of a group who are quite so blessed as golfers in terms of longevity. It's the nature of the game. Of course, being young and athletic is an asset to playing great golf. But at the same time, the diminishing of these qualities does not preclude one from competing at the highest level. Indeed, triumphant tales of veterans whose performances have belied their age litter golf's history books.

There is no finer example than Sam Snead, a sensational golfer in his prime, whose brilliance seemed not to fade with the passing of time. He remains to this day the oldest man ever to win a US Tour event, the Greater Greensboro Open, when he was 52. Some 10 years later he almost won a major championship, finishing third in the 1974 US PGA Championship behind young "whippersnappers" Jack Nicklaus and Lee Trevino. Five years later he broke his age, again in a Tour event, shooting rounds of 67 and 66. Amazingly, he later shot 60 at the age of 71 and, more remarkable still, a score of 66 at the age of 84!

Slammin' Sam was obviously an exceptional case. But there are other instances which still add weight to the argument that like a fine wine, some golfers just get better with age. Roberto de Vincenzo won the Open Championship at the age of 44. Hale

Irwin, already a two-time winner of the US Open, completed the hat-trick when he claimed the title at Medinah at the age of 45. More impressive still, the silky-smooth swinger Julius Boros was 48 when he triumphed in the 1968 US PGA Championship at Pecan Valley. It's nuts when you think about it!

Of course, competing against the young guns doesn't work for everyone. And even those who succeed, except maybe for Snead, do so only occasionally. There simply comes a point when you can no longer turn back the clock.

The great thing is, golf's veterans don't have to nowadays. As the big "five-o" looms large on the horizon, they can comfort themselves with the prospect of the lucrative Seniors Tour. This relatively new initiative has given the 50-plus brigade on both sides of the Atlantic a whole new lease of life. They get to compete against old friends, renew past rivalries, and play a full professional tour schedule. In the United States a place on the Champions Tour, as they call it, is literally a dream ticket.

You might almost say it was launched as a vehicle to keep the great Arnold Palmer in business. That's not strictly the case, but it may as well have been. Palmer was past his playing prime, but he remained an enormous pull both commercially and in terms of his popularity with the fans. The over-50s tour kept Arnie in action and his Army could march again.

Not surprisingly, given the calibre of the players reaching their half-

▲ Argentinean legend Roberto de Vincenzo.

◀ Sam Snead at Carnoustie in 1937. Thirty seven years later he finished third in the US PGA!

▲ Arnold Palmer struggles with his emotions as he finally bows out at the 2004 Masters to end an extraordinary playing career.

centuries simultaneously, it was a winning formula. Even five-time Open champion Peter Thomson, long since tired of the weekly grind of tournament golf, could not resist the gravitational pull of the dollar. In his first year on the US Seniors Tour in 1985 he won nine tournaments and a previously unthinkable $350,000.

In the last 20 years a steady trickle of golf's great players has progressed on to the Seniors Tour, contributing to its rapid growth in popularity and astonishing commercial success. Prize funds are through the roof and incredibly the leading money winner on the US Seniors Tour in recent years has typically amassed more cash than the leading golfer on the men's European Tour.

The European Seniors Tour is a little less grand in stature, with relatively meagre prize money – by US standards, anyway. But it is a highly competitive environment and for many it's meant that life has indeed begun again at 50. Its flagship event, the Senior British Open, enjoys the status of a major championship attracting the best over-50s golfers from around the world.

In recent years, the cream of European golf from the 1980s and early 1990s have hit 50 – including Bernhard Langer, Nick Faldo, Sandy Lyle and Ian Woosnam – which has greatly helped the development of the European Seniors Tour but it is still lagging behind the cash-rich States. It has also been shocked by the illness of Seve Ballesteros. However, there is little doubt that even in these credit-crunching times the seniors' tour will continue to grow.

Away from the pro game, golf has equally life enhancing benefits and gives pleasure to millions who fall into that somewhat vague category of "veteran". It may be a cliché to say that golf is a game for life, but that is undoubtedly one of its main attractions and the reason why we can continue to enjoy it.

All veterans occasionally wish they could hit the ball as far as they used to

and still reach all par-4s with two well-struck blows. But the great thing is, the pleasure of feeling a pure strike – that split-second moment when the ball pings straight out of the middle of the clubface – is something that does not diminish with the passing years. There's no age limit on that kind of fun.

▼ Tom Watson of the USA holds the 2003 Senior British Open trophy.

Women's Golf

► Mary Queen
of Scots playing
golf at St Andrews,
1563.

Mary Queen of Scots was one of the first-known avid women golfers. Indeed, she was possibly a little too keen to indulge in this passion for the game. She was playing golf the day after her husband was murdered, which one would have to say was a little insensitive. Perhaps she just loved golf more than she loved her spouse. Who knows? She wouldn't be the first...or the last!

One thing is certain, this royal patron of the game would be appalled to discover centuries later just how poorly treated women golfers have been, especially in the UK. Admittedly the number of female participants is relatively small compared to their male counterparts, but there is no reason to suggest that this minority is any less keen on the sport. And yet traditionally they have been treated almost as second class citizens. In America, women golfers do have a degree of equality, and indeed, have achieved a freedom that you might say is the envy of their overseas sisters.

At clubs all over the UK it has been perfectly normal for there to be playing restrictions relating to the time of day – or even the day of the week – that women can play. Saturday and Sunday mornings, when any right-minded golfer would love to be out on the golf course, have typically been "men only" tee times. And at some clubs women are even excluded from the clubhouse – or at least certain areas of the clubhouse like "the 19th hole".

It is shameful that golf in this country should have tolerated such discrimination for so many years. Fortunately, times are changing, albeit

◀ Joyce Wethered playing out the rough during the mixed foursomes golf tournament at Worplesden in 1926.

◀◀ Babe Zaharias, one of the game's greats.

slowly, and clubs whose outlooks remain entrenched in the dark ages are increasingly becoming the exception now rather than the norm.

Up until the end of the 19th century, women golfers had grown used to an altogether different type of restriction relating to the clothes they wore. Around this time, bizarrely, swinging the club above shoulder height was considered unladylike. As if they had a choice! Trussed up as they were, it was incredible they didn't do themselves a serious injury.

▶ Michelle Wie
chats with her
caddie during the
first round of the
2008 US Women's
Open.

▶▶ Annika
Sorenstam
playing at the
2008 Canadian
Women's Open.

Players like Joyce Wethered moved the game on in leaps and bounds in the early 20th century, winning championships with such style and athleticism that the great Bobby Jones was prompted to say that "she is the finest golfer I have ever seen". She was an inspiration in the UK, while on the other side of the Atlantic, Babe Zaharias was soon to make her mark in similarly spectacular fashion. It's no exaggeration to say that her impact on the game was no less seismic than that made by Tiger Woods in the mid-1990s.

It's because of trailblazers such as Wethered and Zaharias that the likes

of Louise Suggs and Betsy Rawls excelled. They in turn inspired generations after them, golfers such as Mickey Wright, Judy Rankin and Kathy Whitworth, then JoAnne Carner and Nancy Lopez, followed by Pat Bradley, Beth Daniel, Amy Alcott, Patty Sheehan and Betsy King; they all played their part in moving the game on to ever-higher levels. And today, few would dispute that the women's game is stronger than ever.

Perhaps where the women's game suffers is when people make the mistake of trying to compare it like for like with the men's game. The two are different with neither one "better" than the other. Women don't hit the ball as far as men – at least not until Michelle Wie arrived on the scene! But when you take into account their comparative lack of power, you could argue that women possess equal skill from tee to green. Pound for pound, it's hard to argue that Annika Sorenstam, say, is in any way an inferior golfer to Tiger Woods.

The ironic thing is that while many male golfers wouldn't dream of going to a women's tour event, most could actually learn a lot more there than from studying the likes

▼ Laura Davies talks with Jean Van der Velde during her ill-fated attempt at the men's ANZ Championship event in Australia.

of Tiger Woods and Ernie Els with whom they have virtually nothing in common physically and dynamically. They could no sooner swing the club like them than they could run the 100 metres like Usain Bolt!

Where they can improve is by studying the likes of Lorena Ochoa, Paula Creamer and Annika Sorenstam – fine athletes with exceptionally good golf swings, but without the sheer muscular, explosive power of the leading men. The beautiful, smooth rhythms which characterise their games are something which any golfer, regardless of gender, should wish to emulate far more than trying to smash the cover off the ball.

X-Factor

I t's definitely an oversimplification to say that great golf is all in the mind. But can it be merely coincidence that the world's best players also happen to be the smartest, coolest, clearest thinkers on a golf course? You'd have to say probably not. Indeed, John Jacobs goes as far as to say that the only characteristic great champions share is a "champion's temperament". And, crucially, they're all born with this gift. Call it the X-factor. The mind was the best club in their bag, so to speak.

Peter Thomson was a classic case in point. He won five Open Championships in his career and was the only golfer in the 20th century who managed to win it three times in a row, a remarkable feat he achieved in the years 1954–56.

The amazing thing was, Thomson made winning look like the most

natural task in the world. Others would get jumpy, fritter shots and miss putts. Even the gallery would get palpably more nervous as the tournament reached its tense conclusion. But not Peter. Coming down the final few holes of a major championship he'd be the calmest person on the golf course. He'd walk briskly, almost businesslike, with an unmistakable look of self-assurance. Nearly always he'd be twirling a club in his hands, as if he had nothing much better to do. And he'd use his incredible rhythm, precise shot-making, and

▲ Peter Thomson celebrates his third successive championship victory at Birkdale, 1956.

▶ Jack Nicklaus (left) and Doug Sanders at St Andrews for the 1970 Open, the year Sanders missed that putt.

competent putting to simply close out the job. Another win would be his. The X-factor had played as much a part, if not a greater one, than his ability to strike a golf ball.

Jack Nicklaus was the same. He seemed to live and breathe the words of Kipling, "If you can keep your head, while all around others are losing theirs...". Nothing flustered Jack. He was born with a champion's temperament and he knew, in the moments of intense pressure that was far more important than a fancy-looking swing. Jack expected to win. No one told him that. They didn't need to.

There's more to the so-called X-factor than mere composure, though.

Another compelling psychological element, which actually rings true as much in life as it does in golf, is this; everyone becomes what they think of themselves. Take Tiger Woods. He sees himself as the best player in the world, so that's where he's at. The other thing about Tiger is this; he feeds off the fact that people are intimidated by him. Jack was the same. Neither would admit it. They're both far too gracious to utter such words. But the knowledge is there in the back of their mind.

Obviously Tiger has considerable talent to back-up that mindset, but that self-image should not be underestimated. There have been many exceptionally talented golfers, physically able to hit 99 per cent of the shots Tiger hits, who couldn't hack it on the professional circuit. They probably didn't ever truly believe they belonged there. No matter how often they were told otherwise, it made not a jot of difference. They felt out of their depth...and inevitably they soon sunk without trace.

It's no secret that conquering the six inches between your ears is the greatest challenge in golf. The real debate is this; can we truly change the way we think about ourselves? It is one of the fundamental characteristics about human nature. We'll cover this point again in a later chapter (see Zen), but for the time being let's look at certain characteristics and techniques which almost certainly come naturally to those blessed with the X-factor. Perhaps simply by reading this, subliminally it will exist in your

◄ Tiger Woods striding purposefully at the 2008 Masters.

consciousness and resurface when you need it most – on the last few holes of your most important competition.

Focus on your target

Sounds obvious, this one. But it's amazing how many amateurs lack focus during the 60 seconds or so that it takes to pull the club out of the bag and hit the shot. Some will be thinking about their swing or a conversation they just had with their playing partner. Forget all that. Really get "into your target"

to the exclusion of all other outside influences. Almost let instinct take over.

Develop a consistent pre-shot routine

Most golfers yawn and switch off when the subject of "routines" comes up. But the important thing about a routine is that it keeps you focused. When the best players in the world are playing well, they have what Dr Bob Rotella describes as a "quiet mind". They're just focusing on the target, picturing the ball flight. Even under pressure they have a calm mind. A pre-shot routine can give you that.

Think the same way on every shot

This is the ultimate goal for any player. To be able to stand over every shot from the first tee to the final putt on the 18th and say you thought about and treated every shot the same. It doesn't matter what score you're on, or whether you just had a birdie or a double-bogey, you've got to think the same way on every shot. Once you start to get into

◀ Stewart Cink goes through his pre-shot routine.

that state of mind, you will play a lot better under pressure and have many more consistent scores.

Stay in the present moment

Staying in the present moment helps you hit great shots under pressure. In many ways it goes hand in hand with the principle of thinking the same on every shot. It's about being able to tell yourself that right at this moment, this is the only shot that matters. You're not thinking about whether you're going to break your handicap, whether you'll win the competition. Your mind is simply into playing this one shot.

Yardage Charts

Your typical tour professional would no sooner walk on to the golf course without a yardage chart than he would increase his agent's commission out of the goodness of his heart. As far as equipment goes, it's right up there on the list marked "essential items". Golf bag... check. Clubs... check. Person to carry clubs... check. Ball... check. Yardage chart... check. Pretty much everything else, whilst desirable, they can survive without.

The yardage chart isn't a new innovation. However, in the pro game it has become ever-more detailed over the years. Peer over a caddie's shoulder as he consults with the player and you'll see that the drawings are relatively simple, but that the page is covered in

numbers, providing all the information he could ever need in terms of distances to hazards and landing areas off the tee. In pro tournaments, various coloured dots in the fairway are cross-referenced in the yardage book, to provide distances into the greens.

There's also a separate diagram showing the green itself and the pin position on any given day, always expressed in terms of the yardage from the front of the green and the nearest side. Also, any significant slopes will be clearly marked, enabling the golfer to use the contours of the green to his or her advantage.

All in all, it's an incredible source of information. Not that the caddies have to worry about pacing out all these distances themselves. At each tournament they simply buy a chart from a guy, himself a former pro's caddie, who does the job for them and makes a rather tidy living from the proceeds. Each caddie will then personalise the yardage chart with additional information such as clubs used on each day of the tournament and direction of the prevailing wind.

At club level there may not be quite such attention to detail but yardage

◄◄ Steve Williams studies the ever-important yardage book during the 2004 Dubai Classic.

◄ Bernhard Langer, a stickler for the precise yardage, leaves nothing to chance at the 1995 Open.

charts have filtered down into the amateur ranks and are on sale in most golf club pro shops. These began life, at least in the UK, as simple line drawings on the back of the scorecard, but in recent years have developed into ever-more advanced glossy mini-booklets.

Club golfers have become far more discerning in what they expect from a yardage chart. And in response to that

▲ A spectator at the Masters finds an alternative use for the yardage chart.

demand, more and more golf clubs are now investing in high-quality yardage booklets, which not only give a good first impression to visiting golfers, but more importantly offer them the opportunity to be much better informed concerning distances and any hidden potential hazards.

"1-Up Course Guides", founded by Steven Carr, specialises in what you might call "upmarket" yardage charts. His drawings have a three-dimensional element to them, allowing the golfer to better appreciate the contours of the hole. There's also much more detail, which means it's easy to calculate distances quickly and accurately. Others also now use graphically enhanced aerial photography for more realistic hole representation.

A step on from that, and currently very much in the news following a minor rules revision in 2006, are GPS (Global Positioning System) units which are now available in handheld form as well as the in-buggy versions found at many prestigious clubs. These use the same cutting edge satellite technology as in-car Sat-Nav systems – and military generals – the world over, to let you know exactly where you are on a given hole.

So at any point it's possible to see precisely how far you've hit it, and how far you've got to go either to the green or to clear certain hazards. An unfair advantage say some; natural progress that could help speed up play say others. Either way, the R&A has sat on the fence slightly by allowing committees to create local rules permitting use of distance measuring devices in competitions – but if no such local rule exists, disqualification awaits.

Whether you embrace this new technology or prefer to rely on paper

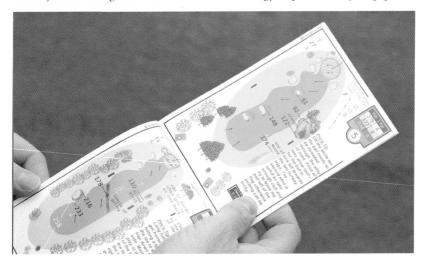

◀ Shot of a typical yardage chart.

and pencil, you should definitely consider carrying a yardage chart if you're not already in the habit of doing so. There are two important factors to bear in mind which will enable you to make the most of these handy little booklets – or gadgets.

First of all, learn how far you hit each club. This might seem a tedious process, but you only have to do it once. And it will make a huge

difference to the way you play and manage your game, as you'll make far fewer tactical errors and misjudgements. So hit 20 or so balls with each club, ideally on a calm day, then pace out the distance to the main cluster of balls, ignoring the longest and shortest five shots. That's how you arrive at your average yardage for that club. Then repeat the process with each club. As we've said, it sounds laborious. But you

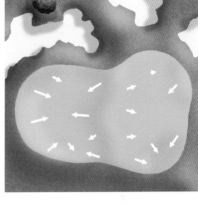

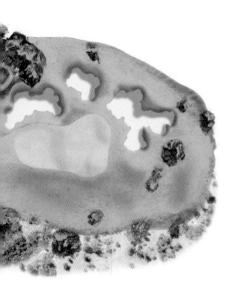

don't have to do it all in one go. Maybe just commit to "measuring" three clubs a week, or something like that.

The second factor is to personalise your yardage chart. The booklets available in all pro shops are of a fairly high standard and, generally speaking, there are plenty of distinguishing marks identifying yardages from around 100 to 200+ yards. However, they tend to be scarcer from inside the 100-yard mark

especially so from 50 yards in. And that's not good enough. Of all the shots where you need an exact yardage, these short-range shots must be at the top of the list as they're all about controlling distance.

So one day when you're playing on your own and the course is quiet, pace out some key yardages within that 100-yard zone, and write them clearly in your yardage chart. Obviously, measure from a permanent distinguishing feature, such as a bunker or tree trunk. You'll then play short pitch shots with a lot more conviction.

"Playing by numbers" certainly has its advantages.

Zen

The Collins English Dictionary describes Zen as, "A Japanese school, of 12th century Chinese origin, teaching that contemplation of one's essential nature to the exclusion of all else is the only way of achieving pure enlightenment".

There's a fine line between X-factor, which we've already covered, and Zen. And it's a blurred line at that. But for the purposes of this book, let's draw a distinction between the two. The X-factor, as we indicated, is something you're born with...or not, as the case may be. Zen is something which can be taught and learned. And if you look at the example being set today in the pro game, you'd have to deduce that everyone's at it. You'll find a sports psychologist, or several, on every practice ground at any PGA Tour and European Tour event. There used to

be a trend towards thanking God in a winner's speech. Now the sports psychologist frequently gets the credit. Divine inspiration just isn't what it used to be.

Look at some of the recent major championships and we can easily pinpoint some examples of this shift. Retief Goosen is one of the most talented ball-strikers of his generation, yet an inherent shyness and pessimism had held him back. He wasn't exactly struggling; he'd won

several tournaments on tour. But he'd have been the first to admit that he was somewhat of an underachiever.

Belgian mind doctor Jos Vanstiphout changed that. He somehow instilled in the quietly-spoken South African a determination and will to win which could not be clouded by negative thoughts. So even when apparent catastrophe struck at the US Open in 2001, when Goosen three-putted from nowhere on the 72nd green to miss claiming the title, he was able to regroup and win the 18-hole play-off the next day. The old Goosen would perhaps have dwelled on the missed opportunity, rather than the one which now presented itself. The old Goosen might not have got into a winning position in the first place.

Compared to Goosen, fellow South African Ernie Els is an altogether different character by nature and probably as far removed from having a weak mind as anyone in the game. Yet even he felt he could benefit from what Vanstiphout had to offer. And you have to say, together they've been a hell of a team. Ernie's playing the golf of his life, winning an average of six tournaments a year since 2001, including the cherished Open Championship in 2002. And

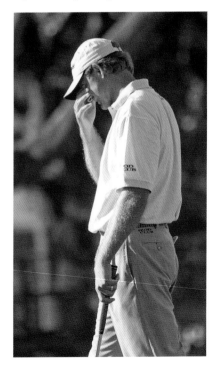

◀◀ Jos Vanstiphout, the number one sports psychologist on the golf circuit.

◀ Retief Goosen misses his second putt on the 18th green during the final round of the 2001 US Open.

▶ Jos with Ernie
Els in 2003.

▶▶ Mike Weir
holing yet another
putt at the 2003
Masters, to force a
play-off.

Vanstiphout's star has gone into orbit, too, courtesy of the Els-link.

Canadian tour pro Mike Weir has also employed the services of a psychologist, a fellow called Dr Rich Gordin. Their approach together was based on introducing clearly defined routines which Mike would adopt on the golf course, to help clear his mind of extraneous thoughts and allow instinct and supreme technique to take over. At the Masters in 2003 it all clicked into place beautifully. On Sunday, when the pressure was at its most intense, Mike's adherence to those pre-planned routines was uncannily consistent. For every full shot he took between 13.7 and 14.9 seconds from walking into the ball to hitting it, a phenomenal skill. Why was this so important? Because the ability to stay with routine means there is less chance of any outside influence affecting your thinking and shot.

It's hard to know exactly what

words are spoken between guru and golfer. Understandably, both parties are reluctant to share such thoughts. It's fair to say, though, that it doesn't involve lying horizontal on a couch or having a watch dangled in front of your eyes and swung back and forth!

Mostly, it probably involves simple mental exercises to try to accentuate the positive thought processes and block out the negative influences; to think about only the present moment and not be concerned about what has just happened, or is about to happen. It can come across as nothing more than common sense; the blindingly obvious, even. Maybe that's partly true. But the fact is, intense pressure can scramble your brain and cause the body to do very strange things. And pressure doesn't get much more intense than trying to win a major championship or PGA Tour event. Recent episodes suggest that, just as you can train your golf swing to perform in a particular way, so too can you encourage the "grey matter" to function almost instinctively in a constructive, positive way.

So how can you achieve your own Zen-like state? Well, probably one of

▲ Dr Karl Morris'
*Train Your Golf
Brain* CD-set.

▶ You'll need your
wits abouts you
for a shot like this!
The treacherous
Par-3 16th at
Cypress Point.

the most annoying things to hear from
someone is "just be positive". No one
tells you how, though. You might start
by promising yourself that you will not
make the mistake committed by a lot
of amateurs who, in the build up to an
important round, tend to think of what
they don't want to do. For instance,
must break 90 or my handicap will
go up to 19. They are already on the
defensive. Turn it around and think
about how low you can go. Play to play
great, rather than playing not to play
badly, as Dr Bob Rotella would say.

You know something, a positive
mindset from the outset will boost
your game.

Other books also available:

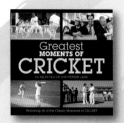

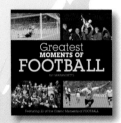

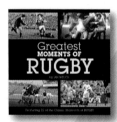

Available from all major stockists

GreenUmbrella Publishing

LITTLE BOOK OF THE
OLYMPICS
AN OLYMPIC A to Z
Written by Jon Stroud

THE LITTLE BOOK OF
HORSERACING
A HORSERACING A to Z
Written by Jimmy Whittaker and Claire Wild

The Little Book of
CRICKET
LEGENDS
RALPH DELLOR and STEPHEN LAMB

The Little Book of
GOLF
LEGENDS
NICK TAPPIN

The Little Book of
FOOTBALL
LEGENDS
GRAHAM BETTS

The Little Book of
RUGBY
LEGENDS
PAUL MORGAN and ALEX MEAD

The Little Book of
GRAND PRIX
LEGENDS
PHILIP RABY

THE LITTLE BOOK OF
EUROPEAN
FOOTBALL
Written by Graham Betts

THE LITTLE BOOK OF
FISHING
A FISHING A to Z
Written by Bob Roberts

THE LITTLE BOOK OF
JANE
AUSTEN

LITTLE BOOK OF THE
BRONTË
SISTERS

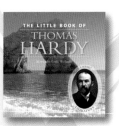

THE LITTLE BOOK OF
THOMAS
HARDY

Available from all major stockists

The pictures in this book were provided courtesy of the following:

GETTY IMAGES
101 Bayham Street, London NW1 0AG

PHIL SHELDON GOLF PICTURE LIBRARY
40 Manor Way, Barnet, Hertfordshire EN5 2JQ

COLORSPORT
The Courtyard, Lynton Road, London N8 8SL

HOBBS GOLF COLLECTION
5 Winston Way, New Ridley, Northumberland NE43 7RF

GOLF MONTHLY
IPC Magazine, King's Reach Tower, London SE1 9LS

GOLF WORLD
EMAP Active, Bushfield House, Orton Centre, Peterborough PE2 5UW

Creative Director: Kevin Gardner

Picture research: Ellie Charleston

Published by Green Umbrella Publishing

Publishers Jules Gammond and Vanessa Gardner

Written by Steve Newell. Updated by Jules Gammond